Sean A Pritchard has a garden design studio based in London and Somerset. He came to his career in garden design with a background in fine art and brand strategy. Before setting up his design practice, Sean graduated with Distinction from the Garden Design School in Bristol. Sean has designed two show gardens for Macmillan Cancer Support, including the Macmillan Legacy Garden at the prestigious RHS Hampton Court Palace Garden Festival in 2022. He divides his time between London and Somerset – where he lives in a 300-year-old farm labourer's cottage on the Mendip Hills, overlooking the Somerset Levels. He applies much of his garden design philosophy to the decoration of his cottage, which he shares on his popular Instagram account, @sean_anthony_pritchard

OUTSIDE IN

A year of growing and displaying

SEAN A. PRITCHARD

MITCHELL BEAZLEY

To Dan – for everything.

'There is scarcely a cottage without some
plants in the window; indeed, the windows
are often so much filled up with them that
the light is too much obscured.'

Gertrude Jekyll, *Old West Surrey*, 1904

CONTENTS

Opposite: Nasturtiums (*Tropaeolum majus*) tumble from a George Bronwin fruit bowl. Through summer and into autumn, hardly a day goes by without there being a display of nasturtiums somewhere in the cottage.

INTRODUCTION

As I write this, there are five very leggy pelargoniums in worn terracotta pots sitting on the windowsill next to me. It's the middle of winter, and for the past week or so the days have been disappointingly grey and dingy – everything trapped in a damp half-light. A clear, frosty morning, when the low sun sends long shadows racing up the surrounding hills, would be a welcome treat any day now.

But, despite my own misgivings, these pelargoniums remain unbothered by the drab weather and are happily shooting towards the ceiling in spindles of leathery green foliage. There are canes now to scaffold the tallest ones. They were sunk into the pots last autumn as the loftiest stems began to collapse – supporting themselves finally became too demanding.

In a few months' time, this windowsill will be transformed. The pelargoniums will have found a new home outside, and in their place will sit treasured ceramic pots that struggle to contain endless nasturtiums in blazing reds and oranges. There may even be a jug of bearded irises – if they haven't gone over already – and perhaps a tiny cup with one or two of the first sweet peas. Colour and perfume will have replaced this monochrome chill: summer changes everything.

* * *

Previous pages: The garden table usually becomes a sort of halfway house for cut flowers before they are displayed indoors.
Opposite: A leggy *Pelargonium* 'Clorinda' in an old terracotta pot is supported by canes in a bedroom at the cottage.

It was spring when I first viewed what would become my home in Somerset, England. I'd spent my twenties living all over London, and always within an easy tube ride of Oxford Circus in the centre of town. But on the cusp of 30, I found myself on a narrow country lane waiting for an estate agent. Hedgerows as tall as I'd ever seen towered above me. They guarded endless open country that was dotted here and there with primroses, red valerian and the remnants of old farm buildings. Birdsong was everywhere. It bounced frenetically around the lanes as tits and finches busied themselves attending to crowded nests. I knew I didn't want to leave the city completely, but I was also craving something slower. Somewhere to breathe, and a garden to fall in love with.

I established a basic history of the cottage some time after moving in. It was built in the late 17th century and belonged to a neighbouring farm as a very modest labourer's cottage. Two extensions followed: another bedroom was added in the 19th century and the kitchen was extended in the early 20th century. As such, the house today is an intimate patchwork of rooms bolted together here and there. Its ceilings are low and the windows are small. Beams jolt at odd angles, floorboards don't quite align properly, and doorways make a failed attempt at being perfectly rectangular.

The cottage being as old and piecemeal as it is somehow lends itself to a quiet anarchism from which I derive a lot of pleasure. I'm not overly fussy about straightening any pictures that find themselves askew on my walls, and I'm not quick to correct a lampshade that's fallen out of position; in fact, I enjoy seeing these inanimate objects behaving like petulant schoolchildren. To me, it brings the house alive, and is, in some way, faithful to the wonderfully imperfect and informal nature of the house. Things land where they land, and there's a tremendous sense of freedom in that.

The main garden is to the front of the cottage on a slope. It sits in a triangle created by two merging lanes that run either side of it. An old stone wall forms the boundary for most of the way, but as the garden starts to end, it's then replaced by hedgerow. It was pleasant enough when I arrived – mostly lawn with the odd shrub here and there – but from the very beginning I knew that more space was desperately needed for planting. I had a dream of creating a jumbled cottage garden; a space that seemed impossibly full and where plants jostled with one another – just like the ones I'd read about in Gertrude Jekyll's books. And so, the lawn had to go. In its place I created large beds that would soon become riots of colour and display all my favourite flowers in endless quantities. Lupins crash against alliums. Foxgloves and hollyhocks rise above hardy geraniums, nepeta and penstemon. Regal lilies and roses

Above: Cow parsley (*Anthriscus sylvestris*) lining the little lane that leads to the cottage in early summer. Opposite: In spring, a rich tapestry of colour is created by planting tulips in large groups across the cottage garden. Here, the pinks of 'Whispering Dream' jostle with the burgundy of 'Amber Glow' and the burnt orange of 'Annie Schilder'.

Opposite: Daffodils on parade in the studio. Displayed rising out of old horticultural show vases, they take on a charming anthropomorphic air of authority – as though they were a line of security guards protecting something precious. Right: Blown-out crocus flowers in little ceramic pots can be found all over the cottage in late winter.

provide the perfume. Later come salvias and dahlias that fire the garden into the depths of autumn. Hard landscaping was kept to an absolute minimum – reserved only for a path and a small seating area – to give every square inch over to plants.

The rooms of the cottage are a kind of stage. A platform for evolving melodramatic performances brought in from the garden. One day it's armfuls of daffodils parading on tabletops, the next it's tulips. There's never a script or even a plan; the plants and flowers improvise their show as they go along.

It's not just about the immediate ornamental appeal that they bring to a room; for me, it is somehow more than that – something more enduring and total. Plants and flowers have become an intrinsic part of the interior decoration, and without them nothing would be the same. Displays made up of mountains of flowers tumbling out of vessels have a way of elevating the cottage; they bring a certain intensity of life and spirit that cannot be replaced with anything else. And, from a more personal perspective, these

displays bring me a deep sense of grounding. They're reassuring connections to moments that remain constant year after year.

My living space continues into the garden. Not in the literal sense (I don't have an old Cecil Beaton-style conservatory overflowing with camellias and pelargoniums – although I wish I did), but in the figurative sense. I want to feel an easy and natural transition between the indoors and the outdoors – as though one were really part of the other. In fact, I suppose I'm on an eternal mission to dismantle any notion of having left the magic of the garden behind when you walk through the door and into the cottage.

Ultimately, that's what this book is all about: the ways in which life can be lived, at all times, as close as possible to the things that we grow. A love letter to the garden and the plants and flowers it brings to the house. All gardens, large or small, have a unique ability to take us out of the everyday and present something of the other to our daily lives – foreign realms that work to their own rules and timetable. Bringing this

Above: *Pelargonium* 'Australian Mystery'. Below: A single stem of *Papaver nudicaule* 'Champagne Bubbles' on a kitchen ledge. Opposite: A display of *Muscari armeniacum* 'Peppermint' in winter.

botanic world inside is, for me, endlessly exciting; it's the slightest sprinkle of anarchy and disorder on a life that is otherwise driven by expectations, deadlines and never-ending administration.

In many ways I'm always looking to capture something that lives in the vivid technicolour of my imagination. A world that has somehow now largely been lost: the gardens in old black-and-white photographs that were the life's work of some enthusiastic plantsperson or cottager. Where annuals were prized and revered, and where large areas of paving were simply unthinkable. Places that slotted perfectly into the surrounding landscape and said something about those who created them.

I'm forever fascinated by the history of cottage gardens and the stories of their owners. My little library is filled with old books that trace these botanical histories, and over the years they have become a comforting escape for me to dip into every now and then. The knowledge and observations that sit within those pages have taught me so much and shaped how I think about the garden and its plants and flowers today. I suppose, in many ways, I owe everything to them: those garden writers, some largely now forgotten, who through nothing more than enthusiasm and a full life in close proximity to plants pioneered new ways of seeing the world around us.

There's a single thread that binds all the chapters that follow together: celebration. Everything I display, both inside and out, comes from a need to celebrate the majesty of colour, scent, shape and texture found within plants and flowers. My life is improved and enhanced immeasurably by them, and, to me, it's unthinkable that a year might go by without filling the insides of the cottage with endless displays of everything the garden has to offer. I indulge the images and ideas that race through my mind – everything a complicated, and sometimes chaotic, reflection of my imagination – and I suppose my hope is that somewhere along the way this book might inspire you, wherever you live, to do the same.

A MUSEUM OF
THE GARDEN

On the kitchen table in early spring any number of things could be going on. If it's the weekend, there may be bowls of vegetables waiting to be peeled, newspapers waiting to be read, and pages of work from the week just gone waiting to be put away. But no matter what comes and goes on that table, there's a constant. An enduring display that remains as life moves around it: a little indoor garden.

I can expect fritillaries leaping from painted cups, daffodils – in huge groups of all kinds – rising from favourite jugs, blown-out crocus falling over the edges of the tiniest bowls, and small terracotta pots packed full of muscari that, when the light catches them, look like glistening oceans. Any other function the table is expected to perform will have no choice but to work around this indoor facsimile of the garden. Within a month it will all have changed. Those same jugs will be a home for drooping tulips, and it will be clouds of cow parsley that are brought indoors by the bucket-load to exhibit in the most prized pots.

But with a *garden* full of flowers, it would be reasonable to ask the question: why?

Opposite: Bright, unruly and endlessly charming: nasturtiums (*Tropaeolum majus*) displayed in an old loving cup by the window in summer.

Why go to the trouble of bringing so much of the garden inside when it can be enjoyed outside in its totality?

I suppose my answer lies somewhere in the deep fascination I have for things being displayed; the idea of a collection of objects that someone has taken the time to curate in such a way that, as a group, they tell a particular story. Displays of objects are around us all the time, but we most often encounter them in a commercial context: products carefully exhibited in shop windows, on roadside billboards and throughout the pages of magazines. The role of the display here is to sell, but, for me, I can trace my interest back to those instances as a child when objects were presented in ways that were intended to inform and instruct.

In school holidays, the best days were always those when my brothers and I would be taken by our parents to the big museums in the city. Those vast monolithic buildings of endless corridors and rooms, where voices bellow and echo if spoken in anything other than a whisper, are the first instances I can remember of being completely captivated by objects laid out on display. There was one room, in the oldest museum in town, that would have me mesmerized for days: a room I now know is referred to as the entomology collection, but back then was simply the room with the insects. It was a colossal space with a mezzanine, cold and always dark, where endless freestanding wooden display cases were positioned along each wall. Inside the glass-fronted cabinets sat the most seductive assortment of butterflies, moths, beetles, spiders and crustaceans, each one seemingly more jam-packed than the last. They were all arranged in perfect rows with each specimen neatly labelled on slips of paper that had started to fade with age, and colour radiated from each display in ways that seemed to light up the darkened room – colours I don't think I'd ever seen anywhere else. I'd spend what felt like hours carefully studying everything.

Being in that room felt terribly exotic. It was a world far away from the one I was used to – a sort of magical cocoon of alien creatures that I could dip in and out of. I'd come home and spend days drawing what I'd seen. I'd be careful to mimic the ways in which they had been displayed in exacting rows. My fascination lay as much in the conscientious way in which they had been presented as in the specimens themselves.

And, although now older and more worldly-wise, that same enchantment at being in a museum has never really left me. That sense of immersion in a place dedicated solely to the discovery and exploration of objects – all thoughtfully packaged and presented to us – still excites me. I think it's the sense of trying to find a bigger purpose or context in the way disparate things are grouped together that really captures my imagination. Collections of insects are interesting, but it's the wider

Opposite: Tulips, as many as will fit, spilling out of a glass jug in spring. Above: *Iris reticulata* 'Clairette', one of the most elegant bulbs to force indoors in the winter. Below: A pumpkin display in the studio after harvest.

significance they take on when formally arranged that, for me, elevates them into displays of wonder and intrigue.

I suppose we're all creating something of a museum in our homes. We accumulate so many decorative things throughout our lives – objects, books, photographs, art, treasured keepsakes – that each adds, in some small part, to the individual story of ourselves, and we display them in our homes like little insights into our lives for anyone that may visit. They say something about us to the world: stacks of books might reveal an interest in wildlife or politics; collections of art may hint at a particular fondness for colour; furniture choices might be indicative of a love for a certain movement in design. Rarely do we display things by accident; every object we place in our home is a calculated and tangible extension of the sparks that light up our imagination, and in this way, we're all curators of our own museum.

Mine is a museum of the garden. Visitors to the cottage will probably be able to glean all the information they need to know about me from the displays of plants and flowers that fill all the rooms. The house is like my own exhibition space for a highly personal show that, although permanent, is ever changing. Collections of colour and texture can be expected; they will sit in groups waiting to be discovered as you move from room to room. Cut flowers tumbling from ceramic vessels will happily coexist with potted plants, and all manner of vegetable crops are also liable to make an appearance. There are little snapshots of the garden everywhere.

Through these indoor displays, I'm hoping to capture something of that excitement I felt as a boy in the room of butterflies and spiders. I want to be him again – discovering the world for the first time. I want to have, all around me, the things that spark a naive sense of child-like inquisitiveness – a feeling that never seems to have fully disappeared as I've got older.

LIFE, DISPLAYED

While it's true that plants and flowers find themselves across all areas of the cottage, there are two places that I am always most keen to see them displayed: in my studio and on the dining table.

These places represent two extremes of the day. The studio is a place of work while the dining table is a place of relaxation, and it's important to me that the two remain quite separate from one another.

Opposite: Inside the studio in high summer there are vibrant nasturtiums (*Tropaeolum majus*), Baltic parsley (*Cenolophium denudatum*), foxgloves (*Digitalis*) and mock orange (*Philadelphus*). A riot of colour and scent.

Overleaf, left: Garden daffodils held by a flower frog in a mantle vase in the studio. Overleaf, right: A collection of violas in winter.

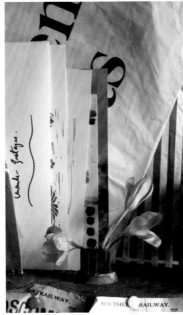

In the studio

It's crucial that I'm surrounded by my most treasured things when working in my studio. This is a highly personal environment, and I fill it from top to bottom with all manner of items that capture my imagination – anything from books, little magazine cuttings and postcards to gifts, bits of fabric and fragments of objects I've dug up from the garden. I like a sort of chaos in there; it's both comforting and grounding to me. My studio is not just a place to work – it seems bigger than that – it's a part of my overall creative experience. It isn't pretty – in fact, it's largely a mess – but everything in it means something to me.

Displaying the best of the garden in the studio adds to this inspiring ensemble. I want to feel as though I've taken my beds and borders and brought them into work with me. In spring I'll display every manner of bulb possible, and in summer there'll be little pots of nasturtiums (*Tropaeolum majus*) alongside jugs of lady's mantle (*Alchemilla mollis*), alliums, foxgloves (*Digitalis purpurea*), calendula (*Calendula officinalis*) and hardy geraniums. They all find a place on my desk and quickly become part of a rotating menagerie of work companions.

One thing I'm really looking for is scent. At times, my studio becomes a kind of garden perfumery with the intoxicating aroma of sweet peas (*Lathyrus odoratus*), roses and mock orange (*Philadelphus*) hanging heavy in the air. Even in winter I'll make sure there's a pot of fragrant forced hyacinths or daffodils by my side. These fragrances calm me and enhance my ability to focus and work immeasurably.

Opposite: A mix of foxgloves, bearded iris and alliums in a favourite cup in the studio. Above, left: *Iris* 'Cat's Eye', a dwarf bearded iris. I find this maroon-coloured bearded iris completely irresistible, and, during its season, there's always one on my desk as I work. Above, right: A tiny display of *Crocus* 'Yellow Mammoth' held in position by a flower frog.

The outside table is an opportunity to celebrate the magic of the garden. Nothing is overthought; instead, the most joyous flowers are thrown together in an informal way. Here, zinnias in bold shades, along with white cosmos and marguerites (*Argyranthemum frutescens*), create an explosion of colour in late summer. Opposite: In late spring, bearded iris, alliums, lupins and foxgloves take centre stage.

Overleaf: Spring tulips (left), and *Rosa* 'Constance Spry' on the table outside in summer (right).

On the dining table

A table prepared for eating with friends is one of those simple pleasures in life that somehow transports you from the everyday into a sort of sensory dreamworld of colour, texture, taste and smell. We leave normal life behind and make a sort of commitment to our tablemates that, for the next hour or two, our attention is fully theirs.

In spring and summer, large parts of my day, like working and eating, move outside, which means that most meals are taken al fresco. From breakfast against a backdrop of happy birdsong to supper stretching long into the evening, I love nothing more than those few months when life migrates into the garden. Not surprising, therefore, that at this time of year most dining displays are put together on outdoor tables. I want these displays to be a continuation of the garden that surrounds them –

I think floating flower heads in an attractive dish look so charming on a dining table. Opposite: A selection of hellebores from the garden are displayed in a little dish in winter – cultivars of *Helleborus* × *hybridus* are my favourites. Right: A collection of amaryllis (*Hippeastrum*) flower heads float on a platter of water. Below right: Garden roses in pinks and apricots on a favourite dish.

overflowing with the same colours, textures and scents growing nearby. Nothing is too over the top: jugs with masses and masses of sweet peas, bowls barely containing an explosion of nasturtiums, vases teeming with multicoloured dahlias – they are all very welcome. And, as far as the food goes, there are always endless courgettes (zucchini), cucumbers, tomatoes and beans in the kitchen garden for tossing into salads with just a dash of homemade vinaigrette. There may even be a handful of strawberries for dessert too.

When the temperature is not quite so congenial and life moves back indoors, attention shifts to dining tables in the cottage. During these colder months, eating with friends feels more intimate, and, as we become ensconced inside, our thoughts turn to hearty soups and casseroles. In winter, the dining table may be decorated simply with a bunch of snowdrops, or a few pots of crocus positioned here and there; I let nature guide me, and I'm just as happy with something sparse and pared back as I am with summer abundance.

CURATING
AN EXHIBITION

Plants and flowers, if you ask me, have the power to elevate any area
of the house, but I suppose there are some specific indoor situations
where their display becomes particularly attractive.

Light

With small windows and low ceilings, rooms at the cottage constantly swing between light and shadow throughout the day. An understanding of how light travels across the house will often influence where I decide to position certain displays of plants and flowers. For instance, on sunny spring evenings, the rooms towards the back of the cottage become illuminated in the most brilliant golden glow and create perfect stages for daffodils. In the same way that a stained-glass window brings moments of multicoloured magic to a dark church, so the low light permeates the daffodils' translucent petals and casts a delicately honeyed filter across everything in the room. In the end, it's about finding those areas inside that, even for the briefest of moments during the day, completely stop me in my tracks as the most ethereal and magical spotlight is shone on the little garden exhibit.

Containment

Some areas of the cottage, particularly in the oldest rooms, are very idiosyncratic to the time in which it was first built. There are nooks and crannies everywhere: mysterious recesses within the walls that once functioned as a bread oven and even an old well that survives in the kitchen from when the cottage was a dairy. I often think these forgotten little spaces are the most interesting areas to position plants and flowers because they add a sense of containment to the display. They frame the exhibits and enclose them in a space that seems purpose-built just for them. Little gaps created on the kitchen dresser or on a bookshelf feel appropriate too – anywhere that provides a platform. I suppose this is the same way that a museum might encase its precious objects in cabinets and cases; they deserve a pedestal from which they can be fully admired.

Surprise

While, of course, plants and flowers end up on tables and windowsills most of the time, for me there is something thrilling about discovering a display somewhere more unexpected. I enjoy displays that sit on decorative chairs or on books piled high from the floor; displays that just about fit onto a shelf or those in a small space that teeter on the edge of being absurd in their grandeur. For me, there's a naivety to these displays of flowers that is both charming and irreverent. A spontaneity that reminds me never to take things too seriously.

Opposite: Late summer on the kitchen dresser: heleniums, rudbeckia, dahlias and zinnias
in an old jug capture the chaos and spontaneity of the garden at this time of year.

IT STARTS WITH
THE GARDEN

Gardens that say something about those who have created them; where planting is diverse, impossibly crowded and, at times, eccentric. Gardens with no tightly mowed lawns or vastly paved driveways. Where on the surface there is chaos, but underneath there is a carefully considered succession of plants that takes the garden from one end of the year to the other. Trends ignored in favour of things that bring personal joy. A place that is the result of the gardener's electric imagination. There is colour and endless fragrance. A patchwork of textures and shapes.

Opposite: Tulip borders in the spring garden.
The delicate, fried-egg colours of 'Antarctica Flame'
bounce through pinks, purples and oranges.

Opposite: In the dark days of winter, one of my favourite jobs is storyboarding the garden for the coming growing season; it gives me a deep sense of satisfaction to feel productive while the garden sleeps. Here, new container displays of daffodils are carefully planned by pinning pictures of different cultivars to a board.

Storyboarding

As with many things in life, to my mind half the fun of the garden and the flower displays it inspires lies in the planning. After all, I was the schoolboy who enjoyed creating revision timetables ahead of exams and the young man at university who had essays meticulously mapped out before any writing began. So I suppose it's no surprise that, now I'm an adult, I continue to find pleasure in preparation.

A large proportion of all the planning I do for the cottage garden revolves around the central idea of indoor display: what do I want to bring inside in early spring? What container displays do I want to see by the back door when I'm in the kitchen in summer? These questions hum around my mind and are released onto large sheets of paper that are then pinned up in my studio. I'll add photographs of things that have worked well in previous years and jot down new ideas as I think of them. The pieces of paper become like storyboards that I constantly refer to and, in many ways, although they look frenzied and chaotic, they bring a greater sense of order and organization to my life than any diary ever could.

The planning pages are useful for me because I like to think of the garden as a sort of performance. I suppose in the same way that a playwright might dictate which characters enter and exit the stage for the best dramatic effect, so too do I direct the flow of the plants and flowers that come to join the drama of the garden.

I wield this power lightly, however. I'm interested in gardens that somehow teeter on the brink of uncontrollable chaos, and, with this in mind, it's important to me that an element of serendipity is encouraged in the unplanned planting combinations which pop up here and there. These storyboards are just the beginning: the start of a creative process that takes me from the darkest depths of winter into the most brilliant uplands of summer.

Cutting flowers and foliage
from the cottage garden

The cottage garden is the main source of everything that I display inside. In fact, if it were not for the irresistible flowers that nearby growers sell at their gates or at the local market in summer, I would have no reason to look anywhere else for display material at any point in the year.

I accomplish this in two ways: planning my garden with cutting in mind and maintaining realistic expectations of what may be available for display at different times throughout the seasons.

The idea that we can have cut roses on demand and lilies in the middle of winter is a symptom of how global supply chains have changed the way we think plants work. Plants are not always 'on'; they're not supposed to look spectacular all the time. They rise and decline with the seasons. They flower and fade. Thrive and die. And yet, despite this, we live in a world where everything is available all at once. It's not only terribly sad to think about the gradual disconnect we've created from the land around us, and how things grow in it, but flying cut flowers around the world is surely so unnecessary in a time of such heightened awareness of the impact our actions have on the environment.

To me, not only is there something deeply unsatisfying about acquiring out-of-season flowers, but there's also a certain ugliness to them too. They are like sterile figurines of their more beautiful selves and carry neither the charm nor excitement that comes from cutting a flower in situ from the garden.

Opposite: The early spring garden displayed in a flower frog. Hellebores, daffodils, grape hyacinths (*Muscari armeniacum*), wallflowers (*Erysimum cheiri*), as well as the snake's head fritillary (*Fritillaria meleagris*) and the purple and yellow *F. michailovskyi*, have been cut from the garden and thrown together with the same wild informality as seen outside. Above: The first bucket of daffodils from the garden in early spring – this is one of the most exciting moments at the start of any new growing season.

How to cut flowers

Early morning is the ideal time to cut flowers from the garden. At this point, plants have benefitted from cooler night-time temperatures and stems are hydrated and plump. Like most gardeners, at the height of summer I'm usually in the garden at dawn; our reward is the extraordinarily clear light that washes over the landscape and the sense of stillness that lingers over everything. At this time of year, there's a great clarity to the garden, and it's usually in these moments that I head out, with a bucket of lukewarm water by my side, and select the flowers for decorating tables and windowsills that day.

Flower conditioning

Conditioning flowers so they stand the best chance of surviving indoors is, I regard, something of a dark art, and one that I think is best learned through trial and error, depending on what you cut most often. If nothing else, with all freshly cut flowers I find it's best to recut the stems at an angle and leave them in a bucket of lukewarm water somewhere cool for at least a couple of hours before using them. As with anything, there are a few exceptions: some flowers and foliage require significantly longer before they become turgid again after cutting – nasturtium leaves are an example, which, in my experience, require an overnight drink before they are ready for display. *Euphorbia* is another example. In spring, I always cut the giant flowers for a large display inside but, in order for them to last any amount of time indoors, it's necessary to sear the cut stems in boiling water for a minute or two immediately after cutting.

Ultimately, the more you cut, the more intuitive you will become about the needs of each individual flower. I have been given, or read, countless advice over the years; some of which has worked for me and some of which hasn't.

Below: A towering collection of Gertrude Jekyll ('Ausbord') roses from the garden. Opposite: Foxgloves (*Digitalis purpurea*) grow informally throughout the cottage garden. For many gardeners, foxgloves are placeholders; they sustain interest between late spring and the fullness of summer. However, to me, they are a star attraction in their own right, and I couldn't imagine the garden or cottage without them.

Succession planning

If, like me, you're interested in using your own garden to supply cut flower material, the key to success is implementing a succession plan.

A succession plan is the order in which new plants arrive to replace something that has died back or been cut for display. This kind of plan serves two purposes: first, it minimizes any obvious gaps in beds and borders and, secondly, it ensures that there's a constant supply of cut flowers throughout the growing season.

Creating a succession plan that works requires a little forethought and an anticipation of how you might cut what is growing. If, for instance, you have echinacea growing through a border that you know you're always tempted to cut, it is a good idea to plant a cut-and-come-again annual – perhaps a zinnia – close by that will pick up any interest lost when the echinacea is brought inside.

Cut-and-come-again plants are ideal for succession planning. They flower profusely and cutting them only encourages the production of more. They're perfect dotted through a bed or border as they prolong interest even when the flowers around them are dying back or are brought inside. Most truly cut-and-come-again plants are annuals, and those that I always gravitate towards include:

- Common marigold (*Calendula officinalis*)
- *Cosmos bipinnatus*
- Dahlia
- Mexican sunflower (*Tithonia rotundifolia*)
- Nasturtium (*Tropaeolum majus*)
- Sweet pea (*Lathyrus odoratus*)
- Tobacco plant (*Nicotiana*)
- *Zinnia elegans*

Opposite: The cottage garden gaining full steam in summer. A jumble of shapes, textures, colour and fragrance.

These plants are among some of the best doers in any garden, but they are all too often overlooked. This is a great shame because they bring so much life to any planting scheme, and most will continue flowering long into the autumn until the first frost.

It can be useful to consider the type of plant you want as a replacement in succession planting. Are you replacing like for like? Or does renewed interest come from a flower that is markedly different from what came before? I always plant a large selection of foxgloves throughout my beds and borders that I can never resist cutting for inside. Knowing this, I'll ensure that I have a healthy number of delphiniums planted nearby ready to spring up and replace the height interest that's lost when the foxgloves are removed. For me, this represents a like-for-like replacement. Foxgloves and delphiniums are both towering plants and have similar cascading flowers. Equally, I'll plant masses of cosmos in areas where I have roses that only flower once a year. This means that even if I cut the roses, or they naturally fade, there's comparable interest to pick up the slack in that area.

Shapes and textures need not always be replaced like for like. In fact, it can be interesting to play with different and unexpected combinations that add variety and contrast to what came before. In one area of the garden at the cottage, ox-eye daises (*Leucanthemum vulgare*) shoot up around fading bearded irises, while Baltic parsley (*Cenolophium denudatum*) emerges through the seedheads of alliums. *Thalictrum* and *Gladiolus communis* subsp. *byzantinus* grow to accompany the purple discs left behind by fading honesty (*Lunaria annua*). Robust dahlias arrive to replace the softness of early summer. In all these cases the plants and flowers that succeed their neighbours offer something different in form and structure, which is not only attractive

Above, left: *Lupinus* 'Masterpiece' growing through alliums and chives.
Above, right: Self-seeded poppies (*Papaver orientale*) in the kitchen garden.
Opposite: The regal lily (*Lilium regale*) beginning to flower in early summer.

for the garden, but also ensures there's an interesting evolution of flowers brought into the cottage too.

Succession planning is particularly important when it comes to spring bulbs. After flowering, the fading foliage of bulbs such as daffodils and tulips should be left undisturbed, so the plants can store energy for the following year. But not only is this foliage unattractive, it also takes up prime space in a bed or border at the start of summer. Therefore, it's a good idea to consider the planting adjacent to the bulbs – what quickly comes next to continue interest in that area? Clump- or mat-forming perennials that appear at the start of summer are a good solution – try plants like lady's mantle (*Alchemilla mollis*) and hardy geraniums which will pop up and cover the ground around them quickly.

Building a garden to provide you with a succession of plants and flowers throughout the season can also involve leaving some elements to chance. I am always amazed every year how some of the most interesting planting combinations are those that have forged a path for themselves with no involvement from me. Allowing plants to self-seed and pop up in the most unexpected of places is, I think, one of the great joys of the garden. Fennel, *Erigeron karvinskianus* and *Orlaya grandiflora* colonize the smallest of gaps in paving; honesty, foxgloves and poppies appear informally across beds; forget-me-nots find an unexpected home among spring perennials; *Alchemilla mollis* is suddenly everywhere. I suppose the key is maintaining a looseness within the planting and not quickly pulling up anything and everything just because it might look untidy. Not only do these intrepid plants bring a feeling of spontaneity and informality to the garden, but they inevitably add to the flowers that are available for inside too.

SOWING A DISPLAY

It's important to me that the garden never stands still, and that there's an element of newness each season to what has been grown before. This not only keeps the outside interesting, but also gives me new opportunities to display different plants and flowers inside the cottage too. For me, one of the most satisfying ways of accomplishing this every year is through the introduction of plants raised from seed.

The opportunities for growing something new from seed are so endless that I often have to stop myself from overindulging in seeds I don't really have time to look after. I particularly enjoy searching for vegetable varieties with an eye out for what might be productive for the kitchen but also attractive if mixed into a border or brought inside (kale, chard and cabbage varieties are usually my go-to for this). Regardless of what it is, there's always something about bringing a new seed packet home that I find so thrilling. I suppose it's a little envelope of exploration and a symbol of something joyous yet to come.

Sowing for me begins in winter when I start on that year's annuals; there's a soothing rhythm to the way this time always comes around again. A school of thought suggests that annuals are best sown in the previous autumn – giving them time to establish and develop while the weather is still mild – but I rarely ever find I have time to do this. Instead, while the weather is freezing outside, I start off in midwinter with sweet peas (*Lathyrus odoratus*) indoors.

When I'm sowing seeds, I find myself entering a sort of deeply meditative state that's difficult to explain. All I can say is that the feeling is one of being at complete peace. I usually have hundreds of seeds to sow at any one time, so I will block out an afternoon, or sometimes even a whole day, to dedicate solely to the task (it's the sort of thing I usually find myself doing on a Sunday with a chicken roasting away in the oven) It's a repetitive activity, admittedly, but I think that's what makes it so therapeutic. It quietens my restless mind.

Opposite, left: Nasturtium seedlings ready for transplanting out into the garden. Opposite, right: Sweet pea seedlings growing on in large containers. Right: Sorting through seed packets.

Housekeeping

Most of the hardy annuals that I sow in winter, such as *Ammi majus*, *Calendula* and sweet peas, benefit from being moved to an unheated greenhouse after they have germinated on a warm windowsill. This prevents them becoming limp and leggy in an environment that is offering warmth but insufficient light. Instead, the cold of the greenhouse encourages root growth and fuller, bushier plants as a result. As a part of this process, there are several things that I ensure are completed every year to give the seedlings the best chance of thriving:

Cleanliness

A highly unglamorous job, especially in the cold of winter, but vitally important nonetheless. At the start of the growing season everything in the greenhouse is removed and all structural elements and glazing (inside and outside) are thoroughly cleaned with disinfectant. Grey mould (*Botrytis cinerea*), which, left unchecked, can rip through the winter greenhouse and destroy all the hard work, thrives in an environment of low temperatures and high humidity, so it's important to eliminate its presence as much as possible. Seed trays that have been in storage from the previous year are also thoroughly disinfected to remove any harmful fungi overwintering in them.

Compost

Seed compost is ordered for sowing because commercial multipurpose potting compost is often too dense and rich in nutrients for seedlings. Instead, they need lots of aeration and drainage for their roots to grow effectively. There's always a certain rush of excitement when I see the seed compost arrive at the cottage: a new garden year is about to begin.

Pricking out and potting on

These two jobs are among my favourites. As with sowing, I find that there's a therapeutic quality to be found in carefully moving seedlings to more spacious homes. Once first sets of 'true leaves' (the second set of leaves to appear after the initial pair of cotyledons) arrive, it's time to search for my dibber, which I seem to lose every year. Pricking out should be conducted with great care to limit the damage to the seedlings' young roots as much as possible. It's a sensitive and delicate job, requiring a more exacting and precise frame of mind than I usually go about my day with. For a few minutes it forces me to shift all my focus to something more vulnerable than myself, and it's this, I think, that makes it so meditative.

It's a special sight through spring and summer when my greenhouse and windowsills throng with developing seedlings. It represents new beginnings and a sense of fresh opportunities – a feeling of nature restored and re-energized. I cannot imagine a growing season without somehow trying to shoehorn one last seed tray onto a windowsill, or the thrill of discovering a forgotten packet of seeds. I find it addictive in the best possible way.

The majority of the plants I sow are annuals and biennials; I suppose, in many ways, the instant gratification becomes part of their appeal. I like to experiment with many different seeds every year, but a core group always consists of:

For flower interest

Ammi majus – hardy annual, sown late winter indoors, with lace-like flowers similar to cow parsley (*Anthriscus sylvestris*) but more delicate. Perfect for weaving through perennials in a mixed border.

Common marigold (*Calendula officinalis*) – hardy annual, sown late winter indoors. 'Snow Princess' (like egg yolks) and 'Neon' (sizzling burned orange) are favourites.

Cosmos bipinnatus – half-hardy annual, sown late winter indoors – in particular 'Double Click Cranberries' (superb purple ruffles) and 'Xanthos' (beautifully delicate lemon-white).

Foxglove (*Digitalis purpurea*) – hardy biennial, sown midsummer outdoors – 'Pam's Choice' (spectacular, white-purple trumpets) and Excelsior Group (a classic showstopper).

Honesty (*Lunaria annua*) – hardy biennial, sown midsummer outdoors, with fragrant, purple or white flowers.

Marigold (*Tagetes*) – half-hardy annual, sown late winter indoors – *T. patula* 'Burning Embers' (red edged with gold) and *T. tenuifolia* 'Tangerine Gem' (deliciously orange).

Mexican sunflower (*Tithonia rotundifolia*) – half-hardy annual, sown late winter indoors, with bright orange flowers.

Nasturtium (*Tropaeolum majus*) – half-hardy annual, sown late winter indoors – 'Jewel of Africa' (a climber with marbled leaves) and 'Black Velvet' (seductively dark).

Orlaya grandiflora – hardy annual, sown late winter indoors, with lace-like, white flowers that look attractive mixed through summer perennials.

Phacelia campanularia – half-hardy annual, sown late winter indoors, with deep blue, geranium-like flowers held high above dark green foliage.

Sunflower (*Helianthus*) – hardy annual, sown late winter indoors – *H. debilis* 'Vanilla Ice' (sorbet yellow-white) and *H. annuus* 'Claret' (deep, purple-red).

Sweet pea (*Lathyrus odoratus*) – hardy annual, sown mid-winter – 'Cupani' (bicoloured classic) and 'Henry Eckford' (explosive red and extraordinarily scented).

Sweet rocket (*Hesperis matronalis*) – hardy biennial, sown midsummer outdoors, with fragrant, lilac flowers.

Tobacco plant (*Nicotiana*) – half-hardy annual, sown late winter indoors – Sensation Mixed (classic with a beautiful fragrance) and 'Lime Green' (refreshing citrus colour).

Wallflowers (*Erysimum cheiri*) – hardy biennial, sown midsummer outdoors – 'Sugar Rush Orange' (stunning sunset colour) and 'Scarlet Bedder' (seductive deep red).

Zinnia elegans – half-hardy annual, sown late winter indoors – 'Envy' (beautiful lime-green) and Oklahoma Mix (prolific and multicoloured).

Ornamental vegetables

Florence fennel (*Foeniculum vulgare* var. *azoricum*) – annual, sown in early summer outdoors. A favourite is 'Romanesco' (wonderfully delicate foliage).

Kale (*Brassica oleracea* Acephala Group) – annual, sown late spring outdoors – in particular 'Nero di Toscana' (dramatic, wonderfully dark leaves).

Swiss chard (*Beta vulgaris* subsp. *cicla* var. *flavescens*) – biennial, sown midsummer outdoors – especially 'Fantasy' (spectacular leaf with ruby red stalk).

Opposite, top left: For me, few things can beat the wonderful simplicity of a little cup of common marigolds (*Calendula officinalis*) in summer.
Top right: *Cosmos bipinnatus* Sonata Series in the garden.
Below left: A self-seeded display of love-in-a mist (*Nigella damascena*).
Below right: A potted pansy on the kitchen dresser in winter.

WILDFLOWERS

At a certain point every spring, I sometimes think I would quite gladly trade all the plants growing in my garden for a wild display of cowslips (*Primula veris*), primroses (*P. vulgaris*), cow parsley (*Anthriscus sylvestris*), red valerian (*Centranthus ruber*), forget-me-nots (*Myosotis sylvatica*), wild garlic or ramsons (*Allium ursinum*), English bluebells (*Hyacinthoides non-scripta*) and orchids. There's something so reassuring about their appearance across the landscape as the days finally ascend towards summer. But I wonder if the enchantment of these wildflowers lies more in their discovery than in their conspicuousness. Stumbling upon a woodland carpeted with bluebells, noticing little bursts of yellow cowslips by the roadside, or finding yourself walking through a field of orchids is such a unique thrill that there's perhaps a risk of overfamiliarity if we were to be surrounded by them all the time.

Happily, the cottage is surrounded by hedgerows and fields that come alive with these wildflowers in spring and summer; in fact, many have found homes in the wilder areas of the garden. They're always a joy to see, and I can never resist cutting one or two for inside. Indoor displays of these wildflowers have an honesty and whimsy that can't be replicated with more traditional garden plants. A bowl of cowslips or primroses is so unassuming that it seems to melt into the objects and furnishings around it – as though the flowers have been growing there all along.

Rules on picking wild flowers vary across the world, so it's important to familiarize yourself with those local to you. Very generally, it's usually fine to pick flowers as long as the plant is not uprooted or disturbed in any other way, is not the subject of a protection order, and is not growing in a municipal area like a park or community garden.

Opposite: In the studio, a towering cowslip is held upright by a flower frog in an old sugar bowl. Above left: Primroses collected from the garden and displayed in a tiny jug. Above right: The lanes around the village throng with cow parsley in early summer. Overleaf: 'Constance Spry' roses in George Bronwin vases as a table centrepiece in summer.

THE INDOOR GARDEN

When I think about favourite times spent at the cottage, I always seem able to recall the flowers that were displayed in those moments. In the same way that specific smells can be so evocative, so the memory of certain plants and flowers has the power to transport me back to another time and place.

These are always happy memories, and they come to me vividly in full technicolour detail. I can trace whole years from start to finish by recalling how plants were displayed in the house, as though their shadow were somehow permanently imprinted on my mind. Flowers have a habit of floating into everything I do, and the opportunity to display them is never ignored. As such, they become a sort of record – a keepsake in my mind – of joyful times spent with those I love.

I suppose there are aspects of everything I do with the cottage – even if I'm not always conscious of them at the time – that have become a part of me and shape how I instinctively think. Enduring themes that frame the way I see plants and flowers inside.

Above: The best of the spring garden thrown together in a small vessel.
Opposite: A selection of foxgloves in a corner of the kitchen.

Drama

Displaying dramatic flowers inside usually requires little effort to make them look good. It could be something tall and imposing like a foxglove (*Digitalis purpurea*) or some cow parsley (*Anthriscus sylvestris*). Or it could be something unusual like a striking new dahlia or bearded iris. I often accentuate the flower's flamboyance by pairing it with a vessel that is modest and straightforward – like a colossal amaryllis rising from a simple terracotta pot, or cut and held upright by a flower frog in a plain white jug. It's a moment of tension followed by a moment of release.

Plants that are not ordinarily regarded as theatrical become so when paired with other things. For example, I might look to a particularly extravagant bowl or a favourite painted cup to display something like snowdrops (*Galanthus nivalis*) or lily of the valley (*Convallaria majalis*); here the drama is created by the peripheral details. I'm also a fan of using books to provide a stage for plants and flowers. It seems to elevate them as if they were on a winner's podium or in front of a crowd giving an important speech. There's a loftiness to it that I find appealing.

Opposite: Cow parsley (*Anthriscus sylvestris*) season always brings high drama to the cottage. Huge stems are gathered to fill the rooms. I want to recreate what's going on in the hedgerow – where nothing is subtle or particularly refined. An exuberant explosion of life. Right: Although small, the spiky daffodil *Narcissus* 'Rip Van Winkle' always seems wonderfully dramatic to me.

Context

Gardens and the plants we display indoors do not exist in a vacuum. As living things, they are connected with the environment around them, thriving and declining depending on the conditions. I always think a good garden or plant display should add something in response to its surroundings; a kind of offering back to the landscape for having taken a piece of it and calling it your own. My garden is very rural and sits on the slopes of hills with rolling countryside visible on all sides. It's important to me that the garden doesn't represent a full stop in this pastoral landscape, but more of a comma. I want there to be a sense of continuity; a sense that this garden belongs to the land beyond its boundaries and I'm merely looking after it for a while. I allow the edges of the garden to grow wild, blurring its frontiers with the encroaching wilderness, and I introduce many of the local wildflowers – cowslips (*Primula veris*), teasels (*Dipsacus fullonum*) and red valerian (*Centranthus ruber*) – into my planting for the same reason. Hard-landscaping elements, like the stone walls that run around sections of the garden, echo those seen in the surrounding fields.

Inside the cottage I treat the plant and flower displays in much the same way. My context is an ancient rural house: there are uneven walls, rooms that lean slightly in odd directions, ceilings that are low and windows that are small. On very overcast days it can feel as though it never really gets light inside – the rooms stuck in a deep and perpetual twilight. In anything I display I want to accentuate all these characteristics. I want plants that lean with the walls and flowers that appear relaxed and effortless. I want to use old ceramic pots and jugs without being fussy about whether some are chipped or too worn. I'm not concerned about perfection or trends; for me, it's always more about honouring the bucolic informality of the cottage.

Above: Nasturtiums, such as the *Tropaeolum majus* 'Red Troika' shown here, just feel right in the cottage. I find they have a naivety and sense of timelessness that complements the age and character of the house. Opposite: For hundreds of years pelargoniums have been celebrated as elegant and sophisticated houseplants. I always prefer them on the slightly leggier side of their growing habit.

Scale

When a flower is particularly tall, such as a delphinium or euphorbia, I love to shine a spotlight on its stature. This is relatively easy for me because the rooms in the cottage are low, and anything of a reasonable height inevitably finds itself touching the ceiling. There's something about the absurdity of choosing to display such large flowers in such low rooms that I love. It's somehow a reminder of the life that is growing outside; a feeling that there's something bigger than all of us – an ambition in nature that cannot be quelled.

These large displays find themselves everywhere, but there are also moments of comparative calm. Tiny displays pepper little shelves and nestle within small recesses on bookcases – like miniature pots of nasturtiums or one or two pelargonium flowers falling from a mini bud vase. Two disorientating extremes that mirror the ways in which plants grow in the garden, and, I think, bring a thrilling energy to the cottage.

Opposite: In winter, tiny cups of snowdrops give the cottage a more sober and restrained feel. They may be small, but their impact on me is huge during the coldest, darkest days of the year. Right: In the hallway, a lofty display of foxgloves is made all the more stately when perched on a pedestal of books.

Left: Daffodils in all their glorious iterations of yellow, white and orange. Opposite: A display of multicoloured tulips in the library. I love them presented in this way, with their different colours and shapes all mixed together. They're made all the more evocative as their stems start to bend and droop. Tulips truly elevate any room in which they find themselves.

Colour

Colours, or shades of colour, often dip in and out of fashion in the garden, with some becoming quite universally reviled. Personally, I tend not to worry about what might be de rigueur, but instead prefer to surround myself with as much full saturated colour as possible. Brilliant yellows, burning oranges, clean greens. These are honest colours – colours that aren't afraid of themselves.

I think it's often assumed that sophistication only comes with something restrained and sober.

Yet, I find there's a playfulness and exuberance to be had in celebrating a full and multicoloured palette. It's the colour seen in the flower paintings of early 20th-century artists like Vanessa Bell, Cedric Morris and Christopher Wood. A spirit of life and a feeling of spontaneity and impulsivity. I suppose I've never really grown-up in that sense, remaining a perpetual child who is still captivated by the brightest colours – those same colours that used to call out to me from the pick-and-mix stand after school.

Scent

Opposite: *Rosa* 'Albertine' in flower in the garden. This rambling rose has a distinctly fruity scent, which is a pleasant contrast to the deeper, more myrrh-infused rose fragrances that appear at the same time. As a once-flowering variety, it has a certain mystique for me. Below: *Lathyrus odoratus* 'Beaujolais' and 'Cupani' still on the vine in a vase. To me, nothing smells better than these sweet peas.

I aim to create little pockets of fragrance inside the cottage that catch you as you pass by – in much the same way they would in the garden. By the kitchen sink, along the hallway, inside my studio and on top of bedside tables: strategic places that I find benefit from a display of scented flowers. In spring, I use these areas as platforms for jonquilla daffodils (*Narcissus jonquilla*); for me, there's nothing better than their intensely sweet perfume. It's a scent so synonymous with the hope and ambition of spring that I want to be surrounded by it all the time. *N*. 'Pipit' is a favourite. In summer, large jugs filled with sweet peas (*Lathyrus odoratus*) are probably my go-to indoor scent diffusers. I display masses of them everywhere; sometimes grouped in single varieties, or sometimes all mixed together in a glorious jumble. The most brilliant perfumes come from the crimson 'King Edward VII' and the irresistible 'Black Knight'.

Scented pelargoniums are also a favourite across the cottage. You need to be a little more tactile with these plants if you are to fully appreciate the fragrance that they largely keep secret. But rub a leaf between your thumb and forefinger and you're rewarded with the most evocative of aromas: an almost savoury smell that's always a joy to discover. There are pelargoniums that go a step further like *Pelargonium* 'Bitter Lemon'. As the name suggests, the leaves of this plant have a strong citrus aroma that transports me to the sun-drenched Italian coast whenever I smell it.

Shape

If a plant or flower has a characteristically distinctive shape, I tend to work with that and accentuate it indoors. In late spring, for example, I enjoy displaying the elongated form of alliums in simple glass bottles – the taller, the better. I dot them across a table to create floral cityscapes and spend days just marvelling at their slender beauty. *Allium hollandicum* 'Purple Sensation' is the classic that you can't go wrong with. Similarly, tulips and hyacinths have a tendency to flop and bend as they age in a vessel – characteristics that I like to highlight.

I usually raise the display above the surface of a table – perhaps with a stack of books – to allow the stems to really droop downwards. I want everything to be natural and uncontrived because, for me, there can be a certain ugliness to flowers that have been overly manicured.

It's also important to me that anything I display inside interacts somehow with other elements and objects in the cottage. The shape of a plant or flower may follow the contours of a lopsided wall, or bend and twist like one of the old beams in the sitting room. Organic shapes that curve, arch and coil.

Left: *Hyacinthus orientalis* 'Delft Blue' falling out of an old mug on the windowsill – just how I like the flowers best. These hyacinths were forced indoors in winter and then cut once they started to droop. Opposite: The unmistakeable shape of *Allium hollandicum* 'Purple Sensation'. The flowers look most effective displayed individually in glass bottles travelling across a table.

Vessel

I find terracotta pots displayed inside the cottage very appealing – especially those with a well-worn patina. To me, the blurring they create between the garden and the house is incredibly satisfying. I hunt them out at flea markets, auctions and from the collections of those who specialize in garden antiques. The thrill of bringing a new one home never fades.

Across the year, terracotta pots are mostly used to display pelargoniums indoors, but in winter they also create homes for forced spring bulbs – like *Iris reticulata* and hyacinths – at which point my windowsills become particularly congested with them.

I'm an obsessive collector of ceramic jugs and cups. I generally prefer those that say something about a time and a place – the more naive and decorative the better – and, as with terracotta pots, I hunt them out at markets and auctions. I look for pieces that are not only aesthetically attractive but also once had a function and were used as such for many years before I found them. I like the idea of repurposing a utilitarian object and elevating it to something altogether fancier with the introduction of flowers.

Of course, I also like to collect vases as well. My favourites tell a story about the maker's personal relationship with displaying flowers. Commissioning an admired potter to create a bespoke vessel is a treat I sometimes afford myself. I want a vase to be a celebration and have personality; I want it to offer something different from everyday life. They are, after all, completely frivolous objects, so why not have some fun with them.

Opposite: Old terracotta pots are one of my favourite things to display in the cottage. They're an interesting echo of the garden; they blur the sense of being inside with outside. Above: A ledge in the kitchen is home to a display of pots, jugs and vases. Displays of vessels like this appear all over the cottage.

I find that bringing together these seven design
elements – drama, context, scale, colour, scent, shape
and vessel – releases a great potential for magic.
There's a story in the personal approach we each
bring to these elements that says something about us
as an individual. We create plant and flower displays
that communicate something of our mood in that
moment, and they become little windows into the
inner workings of our minds. A quiet vulnerability
that we leave dotted around the house.

Opposite: A tiny jug of daffodils on a kitchen shelf – it is
glorious in its simplicity.

PRACTICAL NOTES FOR
INDOOR FLOWER
DISPLAYS

My favourite indoor flower displays are those that happen quite spontaneously. Perhaps something is spotted looking dazzling in the garden and an instant decision is made to bring it inside. Or perhaps you have friends like mine who visit with unexpected handfuls of sweet peas in summer. These impromptu moments of inspiration sustain me and keep a passion for displaying plants and flowers burning throughout the year.

Yet, no matter how offhand the display may be, there remain enduring principles you can follow to help you get the best out of flowers indoors.

Mechanics

If you use an equally diminutive jug or bud vase when displaying small flowers such as snowdrops or nasturtiums, there is usually no need to think about supporting the stems. With everything so compact, the flowers will remain upright, and you simply need to add water to the vessel and pop them inside. Sadly, however, it's not always this straightforward. For larger flowers, like delphiniums and irises, you will have to supply some sort of covert support or scaffolding to keep everything in the desired position.

In floristry circles, floral foam – a lightweight, moisture-absorbent 'brick' – was traditionally used for this purpose; however, this synthetic foam is toxic to the environment. Over time, the foam breaks down into microplastics that ultimately litter the world's oceans. Instead, there are far more sustainable methods to supporting a display:

Opposite: Flower frogs ready for use in the studio. Above: A bowl with chicken wire ready for flowers.

Chicken wire

I've used the same scrunched-up balls of chicken wire to secure displays for years. A little bit goes a long way and will serve you, as it does me, well into the future. In a vessel with a good amount of depth, you can sometimes wedge the ball of chicken wire inside without having to stabilize it any further. However, in shallower jugs and vases a small amount of tape will help to keep the wire in place. Stems can then be placed through the holes in the wire, where they will be held in position.

Flower frogs

These weighted discs have been used to hold flowers in place for hundreds of years. When placed at the bottom of a jug or vase, they provide excellent support for larger stems, and their reusability makes them brilliantly sustainable. I like to collect well-loved examples from flea markets and online auctions, and these serve me just as well today as they would have done when new.

Twigs

Perhaps the ultimate sustainable option, creating a lattice of stacked twigs inside a vessel supports plants in much the same way as chicken wire.

Left: *Iris* 'Benton Olive' displayed simply on a windowsill - one of my all-time favourite flowers to exhibit in this way. Opposite: A riot of late-spring flowers. Standouts include the bright orange poppies, acid-green euphorbias and *Allium hollandicum* 'Purple Sensation' – these colours always look eye-catching together. The display aims to capture the wonderful informality with which these plants grow in the garden. Nothing is thought about too much.

Creating the display

I don't see myself as a florist and nor am I particularly interested in following the 'rules' of floristry. I choose instead to display flowers and foliage in a completely personal way and always in response to how I'm feeling in that moment. My motivation is never to create the most beautiful or prize-winning arrangement; it's more about the sheer joy of displaying what I have grown. I'm inclined to overfill a jug or vase with as many flowers as I can possibly get away with, and I take great pleasure in letting the flowers themselves work out what 'design' to create.

For me, the design of a display is always secondary to the experience of creating it. I fear that if I stop for too long to question how each stem should be positioned, then all the fun and mystique of the process will be lost, and I might never display anything ever again. I'm always trying to replicate a feeling or an atmosphere of something going on in the garden, meaning that I must allow myself to be as loose and spontaneous as the plants outside.

I think we can be too quick to second-guess ourselves when it comes to what is perceived as good taste. Too much good taste is boring anyway; more exciting, I think, is following whatever makes the heart beat a little faster.

DISPLAYING
SPRING

'What an innocent charm there is about many of the true spring flowers. Primroses of many colours are now in bloom, but the prettiest, this year, is a patch of an early blooming white one, grouped with [another of] a delicate lilac.'

Gertrude Jekyll, *Wood & Garden*, 1899

Opposite: Daffodils in spring.

SPRUNG!

There's usually a day when spring creeps up on me unexpectedly. Describing this kind of day is difficult; the arrival of spring is often felt before it's seen. Nothing substantial has changed from the day before, yet somehow there's a feeling, something total and celestial, that today is the day. On this day it seems to me that everything in nature knows it too. The birds seem more vociferous and sunshine pierces through the sky more brilliantly. There's a stillness. Everything is more relaxed, as though thankful to have made it through another winter. The slight chill in the air is not threatening; instead, it carries a promise of days to come that are longer and more productive.

From this day onwards, everything grows, both literally and metaphorically, in intensity. The garden suddenly appears to race forward – each day bringing something new to look at and admire – and everyday life somehow has a fresh purpose. Everywhere you look and in everything you do there's a renewed vigour. There's also that moment somewhere in the middle of spring when very suddenly, almost overnight, the landscape turns very green. Canopies of dense leaves emerge as if from nowhere overhead, while hedgerows explode to twice and then three times their size. On display is a brilliant kind of green, a new and fresh growth so dense that it casts a verdant filter over everything.

Spring is a time of hope fulfilled. A time to celebrate the world around us as it slowly emerges from its winter sleep, and, for me, that manifests itself in the display of spring flowers on every available flat surface in the cottage. The most brilliant daffodils and tulips have now emerged from the bulbs I planted last autumn, and they sit, cut from the garden, in large groups in every room.

We love to talk about the punctuality of our gardens, but assessing whether spring has arrived seems to provoke a special kind of scrutiny – coming, as it does, after the emptiness of winter. But I think the more years I spend gardening and growing flowers, the more I've come to realize that there isn't really a 'normal' by which to judge whether the season is on time, behind schedule or ahead of itself. Every year seems to throw up something different, and really all we're doing is comparing now to the year before. Nowadays, on the whole, I'm more relaxed about the entire thing – the garden will awaken when it's ready and not a moment sooner.

Spring also marks the start of a new season of growing and harvesting edibles. From the first forced rhubarb to the glossy leaves of ruby chard, they not only fill the kitchen with new culinary opportunities, but also create some of my favourite spring displays in the cottage. On the surface there's something quite absurd about presenting vegetables decoratively in

Opposite: Multicoloured tulips, free and expressive, in the sitting room.

Below: A potted display of *Narcissus* 'Pipit' in spring. Being one of the latest flowering daffodils, I use them to extend the season in the garden. I'm always looking to hold on to daffodils for as long as possible. Opposite: Late spring flowers, including *Helleborus × hybridus* cultivars, primroses (*Primula vulgaris*) and the double-flowered *Narcissus* 'Bridal Crown'.

jugs and vases – after all, their main function is to be eaten. However, I find it thrilling to elevate them in this way. Large sticks of rhubarb look like scarlet fireworks as they majestically shoot up out of a pot and globe artichokes have an extraordinarily architectural appeal – especially if left to flower. I'm a big fan of mixing these vegetable crops with perennial planting in a garden border too. It's a play between the decorative and the functional – why can't a plant be both?

Garden jobs increase in their intensity as spring arrives. Before you know it there are seeds to sow, plants to pot up, perennials to feed, things to divide and young plants to harden off. Nowadays, I try not to put too much pressure on myself to complete every job in the garden quickly, and instead take joy in a more leisurely approach to working through the to-do list. However, I admit that I've only recently grown into this state of mind. When I first bought the cottage, and finally had my own garden, I was impatient and keen to do everything in the garden as soon as possible, but this inevitably led to total frustration when I found I almost never had the time to realize my ambitions. Now I'm kinder to myself; it's fine if I'm a bit late sowing something or if I've not got round to cutting something back – our gardens are supposed to be places of joy and freedom. Things can wait.

Of all the transformations that happen in spring, perhaps my favourite is the sudden reawakening of the orchard. Where I live, in England's West Country, orchards have an ancient history, and they have been synonymous with the landscape for centuries. Sadly, their numbers have been rapidly depleted over the last hundred years to make way for development, but luckily many remain in my local area. As the days get longer, the orchard bursts into life. The trees, which have stood silent and naked all winter, prepare for a dramatic change of outfit – cloaking themselves in the most precious white petals. The orchard in full blossom is one of those uniquely thrilling sights of spring that I'll never tire of. For those few weeks I move an old table and chairs under one of the particularly large cider apple trees and try to spend as much time as possible there. I love to display groups of tulips in big pots on the table – their technicolour glory offset by the purity of the surrounding blossom. Like everything in the garden, this time of abundance in the orchard is fleeting: the blossom will fade and will give way to swollen fruits by autumn. Capturing these moments of magic in the garden – and, of course, throughout the cottage – is so important to me. Being truly present and in the moment to breathe in the majesty of spring is something I try to remind myself to do every day during the season. Our lives are chaotic and unpredictable, but spring is always certain.

NOTES ON
DAFFODILS
Narcissus

There are moments throughout the year that I regard as key milestones in the gardening calendar – like the first snowdrops or the first dahlias – but the one that's perhaps most welcome of all is the arrival of daffodils. Planted in autumn, daffodils appear like the most brilliant armies of garden soldiers in early spring. In winter they're the flowers that I'm looking forward to most, and in summer they're the plants I'm most excited to plan for the following year.

There can be some snootiness about daffodils – mainly concerning their colour – that I've never understood. What could be more special than drifts of sparkling, happy faces floating through the garden (and indeed across the countryside) in all manner of bright yellow on an early spring afternoon? Nothing, I'd pledge, is the answer.

Daffodil colours are complex. They arrive in endless yellow-white-orange combinations, and in shades that run from the softest pastels to the most unapologetically saturated tones; I guarantee, there's one for everybody. For those, like me, who are particularly enthusiastic about daffodil growing, the flowers are classified into divisions based on their appearance and given codes that relate to their colouring. There are many thousands of named cultivars, which makes the combination of these divisions and colour codes endless.

My fondness for daffodils is, to some extent, fuelled by their potential for cutting and display. For me, when displayed inside, they are some of the most architectural flowers you can work with. The taller varieties tower high above their vessel, creating a drama that I think is so key to any flower display, and I cannot ever imagine an early spring without masses of them in every room.

I grow daffodils in two ways: in pots and directly in the ground. I display both pots and cut flowers inside the house. I sit the potted varieties on old plates and place these on top of stacks of books by sunny windows, and the daffodils I've cut from the ground find themselves in all manner of jugs and vases – with usually one too many crammed in. Once indoors, they move around the cottage depending on where I think they look best that day.

I tend to be drawn to daffodils that produce very tall flowers like 'My Story' and 'Cornish King'. There are, of course, smaller favourites, such as 'Elka' and 'Rip Van Winkle', but, generally, I want daffodils to interact with objects in the cottage by rising above them. I want a display that collides with

Opposite: A bucket of mixed daffodils brought in from the garden in early spring. Something I never get bored of.

Opposite: Inside, I mostly prefer to display daffodil varieties all jumbled together in a jug. Their mix of colours and shapes looks like little fireworks to me. Here, in the library, they cut through the half-light of dawn. Above, left: *Narcissus* 'Eaton Song' growing in the garden. Above, right: *Narcissus* 'Bella Estrella'.

pictures on the wall and that just about touches a beamed ceiling when placed on a high bookshelf.

Out in the garden the opportunities for daffodils are endless. I think they look particularly attractive planted in containers – where, again, I tend to opt for taller varieties – but also creating drifts through a lawn or border always looks so charming. The great advantage of daffodils over the later tulips is that, once established, they are perennial and will continue to return with their display year after year.

Selecting daffodil bulbs

Daffodil bulbs are widely available from late summer in supermarkets and homeware stores. They are usually sold in large sacks of the more common varieties – which is perfectly fine – however, for a greater choice, specialist bulb nurseries are the place to go. These nurseries usually supply via mail order and stock an endless range of exciting and unusual varieties. Nowadays, I purchase several new ones every year in this way, but if you're just starting with daffodils, it's worth investing in a broad selection of colours and shapes that you find attractive.

Local daffodil societies are a useful source of advice too. If, like me, you find yourself becoming somewhat addicted to daffodil growing, these societies are a perfect place to engage with others who have many years' experience and will be able to advise on the best places to source bulbs locally. These groups can seem intimidating when you're just starting out, but amateur growers of flowers are almost always an exceptionally friendly bunch, so you needn't worry.

Planting daffodil bulbs

Daffodil planting should be completed by early autumn. Daffodils need a long period to establish their roots over winter, so it's best to prioritize this job at the first sign of summer coming to an end. This does mean that bulb orders from specialist nurseries need to be placed earlier than you think if they are to arrive in time. I generally start planning my order for the following year just after the daffodils go over in late spring – but this may be a tad early for some.

I usually create single displays of the same daffodil variety in terracotta pots that are at least 33–35cm (13–14in) in diameter. For pots this size I plant around ten bulbs for the fullest display, but in the ground I tend to stick to clumps of around five to six bulbs to give them space to naturalize and spread.

Containers are filled a little more than halfway with a multipurpose potting compost that I mix with a small amount of horticultural grit. The bulbs are placed on top and then covered with the same compost–grit mix. To finish, I always add a final top layer of horticultural grit: it not only looks a bit smarter, but also prevents the stems getting dirty from splashback when it rains in the flowering period. Once this is done, the pots are left undisturbed until spring.

Daffodils in flower

I like to extend my daffodil displays by planting a mix of early, mid- and late-season varieties. From the very earliest days of spring it's possible to have daffodils in bloom for a good two to three months if you select cultivars that flower at different times. A good starting mix is:

Early season	Mid-season	Late season
'Early Bride'	'Cornish King'	'Bella Estrella'
'Ice Follies'	'Fortune'	'Pipit'
'Rip Van Winkle'	'Golden Echo'	'Replete'
	'Tahiti'	'Tommy's White'

Top: *Narcissus* 'Altruist' in the garden. Above: *Narcissus* 'Golden Echo' is always a favourite. Opposite: There are so many different shapes and colours of daffodil that it's impossible to get bored of them. Spring in my garden, and indeed in the cottage, would not be the same without them.

After flowering

Deadhead any spent daffodil flowers but leave the bulb and its leaves in place to die back naturally. This is crucial because the retreating foliage goes on to feed the bulb for the following year's growth. Once the leaves have finally died back, I tend to plant any bulbs grown in containers out in the garden – although they will continue to flower for years in a pot if the compost above the bulb is replaced every season.

Favourite daffodils to display

'Bella Estrella'

'Bella Estrella' is a Split-corona daffodil, which means that its trumpet centre has an attractively disjointed, almost frilly appearance. This variety has milky petals and a yolk-yellow centre, making it the perfect 'fried-egg daffodil'. After all the early varieties have flowered, 'Bella Estrella' comes along with mid-season extravagance. The flowers shine in containers and their unusual appearance adds a certain curiosity to any wider display. Flowering on good-sized stems, I use them in a mixed group of cut daffodils where they stand out and add a different kind of texture. Height: 35cm (14in).

'Fragrant Breeze'

As the name suggests, 'Fragrant Breeze' has the most deliciously sweet scent, which is highly welcome early in the season when this daffodil flowers. I cut the flowers ferociously to display around the cottage – hoping to catch moments of their perfume as I move from room to room. This is a Large-cupped daffodil, which means the apricot-yellow corona is more than one-third the size of the surrounding pure white petals. Height: 40cm (16in).

'Golden Echo'

It's a close race but I think 'Golden Echo' is one of the most beautiful daffodils you can grow. Small, milky white petals melt into butter-yellow centres late in the season above slender, reed-like foliage. It's a Jonquilla daffodil, which means it has more than one flower per stem and a gloriously delicate perfume. I always have a few potted displays of 'Golden Echo' in the garden, and they become the flowers that I gravitate to first when looking for daffodils to display inside. They have a real elegance and sophistication – everyone should grow them! Height: 30cm (12in).

'Rip Van Winkle'

A Double daffodil, 'Rip Van Winkle' produces a striking spiky flower early in the season. An heirloom variety, introduced in the 19th century, it never fails to surprise me. It looks a little like a cactus dahlia with swirling, bright yellow petals on short stems. I only ever really display 'Rip Van Winkle' in containers as, for me, lifting these flowers off the ground and into their own space is where they look their best. I cut masses of them to display inside. As a more diminutive daffodil, it looks charming in smaller jugs and cups. Height: 15cm (6in).

'Tresamble'

'Tresamble' daffodils are something of a palette cleanser mid-season. Popping up delicately on slightly smaller stems to most other varieties, the pure white flowers look incredibly elegant in any spring display. 'Tresamble' is considered an heirloom variety, predating 1930, and is classed as a Triandrus daffodil. This means that the flowers are multiheaded and point downwards with reflexed petals – as though happily nodding. This is a superb daffodil to plant in drifts around the garden, and it also works well cut for indoors as a slightly calmer alternative to its more extravagant peers. Height: 30–40cm (12–16in).

Opposite, from top to bottom: 'Golden Echo', 'Rip Van Winkle', 'Tresamble', 'Fragrant Breeze' and 'Bella Estrella'.

A cottage full of daffodils

It's a special kind of feeling to wake up in the morning and know that outside the daffodils are, finally, all in flower. That may perhaps sound dramatic, but after a winter watching the slow growth of their slender, sword-like leaves, to finally have them open feels like the bombastic climax to a performance that's been gradually building in drama and suspense. They're collected from the garden – ten or more at a time – and found new homes on tables and windowsills. Everyday jobs around the cottage become more pleasant just because they are there.

The faces of daffodils shine. They sit inquisitively in their vessels as if a small crowd has developed in the house and become curious about what is going on inside – a little audience that watches me as I go about my day.

Daffodils bring a sweet perfume into the cottage. It's never as overwhelming as the ones that are forced inside in pots over winter, but they do, nonetheless, throw little hints of spring fragrance here and there. I'll walk past a jug of them in the kitchen and press my face up close every now and then. For a few moments that hit of perfume transports me to a fantasy kind of spring. A spring that's endless in its sunshine and sparkling birdsong.

I forget that for most of the year they aren't around. They feel so perfect and slot into the character of the cottage so well that, while they're here, it's hard to believe I ever live without them. They motivate me. They make me want to paint a room in bright yellow and buy hundreds of little jugs that could display every last one individually. They're addictive, and they make me question, every year, why I didn't plant more of them.

I feel a genuine sort of heartbreak as the last ones start to fade in the cottage. Those vibrant happy faces become dry and begin to shrivel, and there are none left in the garden to replace them. Everything suddenly feels as though it's going too quickly; I'm two steps behind spring and I want it to slow down. They've been and gone. Rooms are now full of tulips. But the daffodils' legacy of a new season born lives on all around the cottage.

Above: A cup of the earliest daffodils with rhubarb leaves at the very start of spring. Opposite: A little corner with a display of daffodils. As winter turns to spring, the days can sometimes remain disappointingly dark and dull. Yet displays like this are a constant reminder of the glorious light and colour still to come.

NOTES ON
TULIPS
Tulipa

After daffodils the spring garden really starts to get going with the arrival of tulips. Tulips are quite different from daffodils in pretty much every way except for the fact that they both start life as bulbs. Where daffodils stand strong and upright, tulips bend and droop. Where daffodils open to reveal themselves, tulip flowers remain closed and secretive for a longer period. Where daffodils come in a colour palette of yellows, whites and oranges; tulips know no such boundaries, and prefer instead to indulge in all the shades of the rainbow.

It figures, therefore, that I use tulips in a different way to daffodils for indoor display. If daffodils are architectural and statuesque in the cottage, I want tulips to dance, to rise and fall, and to burst with colour. I want riots of tulips everywhere.

For me, I suppose a large part of the appeal of tulips lies in their wonderful ability to make a bold statement indoors – how when they're cut and displayed, they take on something of the character of the space in which they sit. Tulips grow into the room. They move and twist towards the light. Their colours bounce around objects and furniture. Tulips simply have an uncanny ability to elevate the interior decoration.

I pack as many tulips as I can into a jug, stabilizing them with chicken wire or a flower frog, then let them do their own thing. I place them on top of books or within little nooks and crannies. I sometimes use glass vessels, especially for the taller varieties, as I find seeing the whole stem – how it bends to support the blousy flowers – incredibly evocative.

I treat tulips as annuals and plant them in both containers and in the ground. Most tulips rarely put on as good a show after their first year of flowering, which means new bulbs need to be planted each autumn to maintain a show-stopping display. In this respect, they're more high maintenance than other spring bulbs – which tend to be predominantly perennial – but the extra effort is always worth it. There are exceptions to this, though: 'Spring Green' and 'Pink Impression' are two tulip varieties that I've found to be more perennial than others and can be left in situ in the garden for a satisfying recurring display. There's also the fascinating world of species tulips – all of which are truly perennial. Unlike most of the tulips we're familiar with, species tulips are unhybridized and have quite a different look and feel. They're smaller, more delicate and less outrageously coloured, but have a charm of their own. These bulbs

Opposite: A tulipiere that I commissioned my dear friend Colette Woods to design and produce for the cottage is populated by the longest tulip stems.

Below: Tulips after cutting in spring. Opposite: Tulips growing across the garden and *Tulipa clusiana* var. *stellata* displayed in the library. As a species tulip, this flowers each year. Species tulips are some of the best to display inside, as they bend and droop into shapes that are often very dramatic.

will happily naturalize and return year after year, making them a less time-intensive (and expensive) solution to tulip growing. My favourites are *Tulipa clusiana* 'Cynthia' and *T. clusiana* 'Lady Jane'.

Selecting tulip bulbs

As with daffodils, the more interesting tulips are usually found at specialist bulb nurseries. Tulips should be planted later in the autumn than daffodils – ideally after the ground has experienced a hard frost. Therefore, if you order tulip bulbs alongside daffodil bulbs, you'll need to consider how you plan to store the tulip bulbs until it's time to plant. Tulip bulbs should be kept somewhere cool and ventilated to avoid the risk of rotting and they also need to be protected from mice.

Planting tulip bulbs

Treating tulips as annuals means that I plant them in the garden more densely than I would any other bulb – I'm looking for an instant hit that's both full and celebratory. I'm of the opinion that the more you plant in a drift through the garden, the better.

Plant the bulbs fairly deeply in a hole with a depth roughly three times their size and leave around 5cm (2in) between each one. In the ground I prefer to grow a multicoloured display of different tulip varieties mixed together, but in containers, I plant them much like I plant daffodils – around ten bulbs of one variety to a 33–35cm (13–14in) pot.

Tulips in flower

The tulip season can be extended by planting a mix of bulbs that flower at different times. The species *T. clusiana* 'Cynthia' is particularly early (and usually flowering before most other tulips in my garden), while *T.* 'Ayaan' is one of the last and hangs around much longer than anything else. For a spread of tulips at either end of the season, a good starting point is:

Early season
T. 'Candy Prince'
T. clusiana 'Cynthia'
T. 'Van der Neer'

Late season
T. 'Angélique'
T. 'Ayaan'
T. 'Carnaval de Nice'
T. 'Yosemite'

Favourite tulips to display

'Annie Schilder'

'Annie Schilder' emerges later in the season like a precious jewel of fiery orange. The goblet-shaped flower has the slightest flush of pink through the petals that tempers the orange a little but doesn't reduce any of the vibrancy. This is one of those bright tulips that I love to display indoors – its boldness so alluring in the dark light of the cottage – and it flowers on a good-sized stem, making it perfect for cutting. 'Annie Schilder' is classed as a Triumph tulip: a classic, goblet-shaped, single flower on strong, robust stems. A real delight. Height: 45cm (18in).

'Aphrodite'

I can never have enough pink tulips, and 'Aphrodite' is one of the best. The flower is a two-tone pink with a darker flame-like flash running up the side of each petal. The flower opens into a perfect saucer shape held elegantly on a strong stem. 'Aphrodite' is a Single Early tulip which, as the name suggests, means that it produces single flowers early in the season. It has interesting foliage with an ivory-white edge to each leaf. This makes it a good choice for containers where the whole plant can be admired. For more glorious pink, try 'Kansas Proud'. Height: 45cm (18in).

'Chansonette'

'Chansonette' is an incredibly elegant Triumph tulip with a perfectly curved shape and pointed petals. Its flowers are an irresistible deep purple with creamy white borders somewhat reminiscent of a candy bar. It has an overall grace and sense of splendour that makes it so charming to display in the garden and cut for indoors. In my experience, 'Chansonette' flowers later than a lot of other tulips – prolonging the tulip display well into the latter stages of spring. Height: 40cm (16in).

'Spring Green'

You often hear gardeners talking about good doers and, for me, the 'Spring Green' tulip is one of them. Unlike most other tulips, 'Spring Green' seems to return year after year just as vigorously as the first time it flowered – I have a great clump of them in my garden that I've left undisturbed for several years. It is the most brilliant, almost translucent, white with splashes of vibrant green running up each petal (this touch of green is characteristic of the Viridiflora group of which it's a member). 'Spring Green' grows tall and, despite its muted colours, makes a real statement. There's something very magical about this tulip; it has an almost mythical quality that I adore. Height: 50cm (20in).

'Grand Perfection'

Perhaps my all-time favourite, 'Grand Perfection' is a classic rhubarb-and-custard coloured tulip, and it's as enchanting to me now as it was when I first started to grow it many years ago. This tulip is reminiscent of those sumptuous flowers depicted in paintings by 17th-century Dutch Masters – with ruby-red flames engulfing custard-coloured petals. Inside, I like to display the flowers in large groups spilling out of old urns and bowls, just as those Dutch artists painted them. 'Grand Perfection' is another Triumph tulip that stands regally on strong stems. Height: 45cm (18in).

'Amazing Parrot'

I have a love–hate relationship with Parrot tulips. There are some that I adore and others that I dislike. Perhaps I haven't given enough of them a chance in the garden; I only ever grow one or two varieties each year. One that I have found myself returning to is 'Amazing Parrot'. It's a very late tulip and flowers in my garden as alliums and foxgloves are starting to appear at the start of summer, making it an incredibly valuable splash of colour after all the other tulips have gone over. The flowers are a sort of frenzied mix of pink, orange and yellow, and, in keeping with the Parrot group, the petals are curiously ruffled at the edges. The eccentricity of its shape makes it a perfect companion for the bearded iris in flower at the same time. Height: 40cm (16in).

Opposite: Tulips in a range of
jewel-like colours bending into the
shadows of the hallway. Tulips have an
uncanny ability to elevate these dark
areas into little pockets of intrigue.

A cottage full of tulips

Cutting tulips from the garden early in the morning feels like such a great indulgence. How perfectly has nature spun its magic that I might be out under hazy dawn sunshine collecting such multicoloured treasures. On the best bright mornings tulips seem to create the most exotic carpet of sparkling pinks, purples, reds and oranges. They're upright, tight and rigid, but soon, in the cottage, they'll transform into mischievous dancers, as they twist, droop and drop their petals.

There are corners of the cottage where dark shadows are cast for most of the day. Little forgotten alcoves that exist in a permanent kind of twilight. I find that tulips work best in these areas. Their colours seem to penetrate the half-light and shine as brilliantly as they would if illuminated by a clear spring sky. They contort and twist into the shadows. Their flowers open wide before their petals drop to the tabletop and then to the floor. It's a drama played out in the gloom.

No other flower seems to work quite so well in these dark areas of the cottage. Nothing else has the intrigue and the mystery that tulips bring to them. Their indoor performance lifts the dullest of days and the most subdued of my moods.

Buckets and buckets of tulips are brought into the house from the garden. There's no space left really; everywhere is already bejewelled by them. But, somewhere, another jug and another bit of space is found. It's impossible to resist.

Tulip petals scatter the floorboards and carpets like confetti, the stamens like little arrows fired from a crossbow here and there. I'm not quick to sweep them away; they're too beautiful for that, so they remain randomly strewn for a moment. Eventually, the tulips have exhausted themselves and it's all over. The dark corners of the cottage become empty once again, and all that remains are the plans swirling round my head of different varieties to try next year and the new ways I might plant them in the garden and display them in the cottage.

NOTES ON
BEARDED IRISES
Iris germanica

Just when I think we're in the swing of the growing season, there's always a sudden lull in flowering after the tulips have finished in mid- to late spring. Most perennials aren't quite out yet, and the hellebores and fritillaries that provide early interest are dying back. Penstemons, alliums, lady's mantle (*Alchemilla mollis*), roses, foxgloves and delphiniums are all so nearly ready to shine, but appear to be taking one last deep breath before the chaos of summer begins.

There is, however, always one plant that I can rely on to single-handedly bridge this gap. A flower so special that clearly everything else knows better than to try and steal its spotlight. It's the jewel of late spring: the bearded iris (*Iris germanica*).

If ever there was a flower that looked as though it had come straight from the canvas of a painting, it must surely be the bearded iris. Frilly petals that swirl and contort in every possible colour, as though created by the frantic turn of a brush. In my mind they sometimes get lost in the feverish anticipation of the daffodils and tulips, but, once the bearded irises arrive, they remind me that they're every bit as majestic and thrilling as their earlier spring peers.

Vita Sackville-West, the celebrated plantswoman who brought the glorious gardens at Sissinghurst to life, was a major champion of bearded irises. She planted huge swathes of them at Sissinghurst, which lined pathways and popped up through the various garden 'rooms' she created. The display is maintained today, making the garden worth a visit in late spring – I certainly think I can trace my fondness for bearded iris back to these displays. I'm also forever fascinated by the cultivars that artist, plantsman and personal hero Cedric Morris bred at Benton End, his home in Suffolk, throughout the 20th century. To me, there's something about the way he painted them – the way they were displayed in large groups rising in full magnificent detail out of jugs and vases that forever captures my imagination.

Bearded iris are classified as those with petals arranged in standards and falls. Intuitively, the standards stand upright and the falls point downward. A mix of the two petals combines to create the iconic flower shape for which they have become so well loved. The 'beard' refers to the fluffy, caterpillar-like appendage that sits at the base of each fall.

Opposite: A collection of bearded irises (*Iris germanica*)
held in a favourite bowl with a flower frog.

Above, left: Unlike most of the bearded irises in my garden, this is not a Cedric Morris variety. It is one of the first bearded irises I ever planted, and, sadly, I've long lost the label and have forgotten its name. But nevertheless, I absolutely adore it every late spring when it reappears. Above, right: *Iris* 'Benton Daphne'. Opposite, left: *Iris* 'Benton Pearl'. Opposite, right: *Iris* 'Benton Olive'.

Planting bearded irises

Bearded irises grow from rhizomes that thrive when they are baked in summer sun, so are ideally planted from midsummer to mid-autumn. For this reason, it's important that the rhizome is planted so it sits slightly proud of the soil. They should be positioned in the sunniest spot in the garden, and in spaces where foliage from other plants won't restrict the amount of sunshine penetrating the rhizome at ground level.

Bearded irises in flower

I tend to mix bearded irises through a bed of late-spring perennials while trying to ensure that the rhizomes aren't too shaded by everything else growing around them. If my collection were larger, I suppose I would consider giving them a bed all to themselves, yet, as it is, they pop up and grow through delphiniums, lupins and foxgloves.

The Cedric Morris cultivars are perhaps my favourite for the cottage garden – purely for the way they engage me in daydreams about life at Benton End and the art school he founded there. Four in particular that I look forward to every year are:

'Benton Caramel'
This is a stunning bearded iris and should be the first to go in any garden. Its standards are a delicate pink and the falls a sort of Beaujolais-red, from which extend a striking, bright orange beard. Height: approx. 90cm (35in).

'Benton Daphne'
Just sublime in every way. The standards and falls are a soft pink that fades to creamy yellow at the centre. It's blousy and yet sophisticated. When it rises from the cottage planting, it takes my breath away. Height: 80cm (32in).

'Benton Lorna'
This is a very pretty, two-tone iris with violet standards and ivory falls that are brushed at the edges with splashes of purple. A yellow beard supplies a striking contrast. Height: approx. 1m (3ft).

'Benton Olive'
Butter-yellow standards and creamy falls with violet centres. Height: approx. 70cm (28in).

Top: *Iris* 'Benton Menace' in the garden. Above: *Iris* 'Benton Lorna'. Opposite: My favourite way to display bearded irises is the one used by artist Cedric Morris when he was painting them. They rise in multicoloured groups from bowls, like rockets heading for space. Here, they are accompanied by a handful of alliums and the delicate flowers of *Narcissus* 'Tommy's White'.

After flowering

Deadhead any spent flowers to encourage the possibility of a second flush (although this only ever happens very occasionally in my garden). In autumn, cutting back the foliage to around 15cm (6in) not only makes the plant look a little smarter over the winter, but also reduces the risk of diseases that overwinter on the leaves.

Every three years it's a good idea to divide clumps of rhizomes to encourage more vigorous growth and increase your stocks of the plant. Lift the iris after flowering and cut away any young, healthy rhizomes from the clump (retaining as much of the rhizome roots as possible). You'll probably notice the central rhizome has become tough and woody. This can be discarded since its ability to flower healthily will only diminish over time. Then replant the healthy rhizomes, ensuring they are exposed, and cut back any foliage to maintain the plants' stability in strong winds.

A cottage full of bearded irises

I like to display bearded irises in the cottage in much the same way I display daffodils. They stand upright and stately and, I think, look best on their own – or at the very most mixed with one or two of the very late daffodils that are still hanging around the garden. Large, multicoloured groups of them tower out of bowls or vases.

Bearded irises sit, majestically, on tables like prized jewels, and when the sunshine catches them in just the right way they take on a magical sort of translucency that somehow amplifies the wonderful eccentricity of their shape. They make me feel closer to the heroes and people I admire who enthused about them long before I came around to them.

These irises are a much more sought-after flower in my garden, as I don't grow them in anywhere near the same numbers as tulips and daffodils – something, I know, I must fix immediately. This does mean, however, that each one is given a special sort of attention and adulation when it finds itself inside the house.

The appearance of bearded irises in the cottage means that summer is moments away. Everything is about to flower with a huge bang. They represent one last moment of a quiet and gentle spring.

SPRING
INSIDE THE COTTAGE

The cottage in spring turns into a gallery of everything going on outside. A new dawn: a fresh opportunity to celebrate the garden. Nothing stays where it was first placed. Everything is on permanent rotation depending on how I'm feeling, what the light is doing or whether guests are expected. It's a big spring moveable feast. Aside from daffodils, tulips and bearded irises, there are other spring stalwarts that always find themselves inside and are worthy of noting here:

Bulbs

Fritillaries, particularly *Fritillaria acmopetala*, and grape hyacinths *Muscari armeniacum* 'Valerie Finnis' and 'Peppermint' (two favourites), are often found scattered across various tables early in the season.

Columbine (*Aquilegia*)

No cottage garden would be complete without little cameos here and there of self-seeded *Aquilegia* – they pop up in my garden just as the daffodils and tulips are fading. It's always so charming to see their delicately bobbing heads rising above forget-me-nots (*Myosotis scorpioides*) and clumps of *Euphorbia amygdaloides* var. *robbiae* as spring really gets going. There's always a selection I cut for the house that are usually displayed simply, on their own, in an old bowl or jug.

Cow parsley (*Anthriscus sylvestris*)

This grows in glorious abundance along the hedgerows that surround the cottage and looks fantastic brought inside in huge clumps – the bigger, the better.

Hellebores (*Helleborus*)

I have a collection of hellebores in my garden that flower for long periods from late winter to late spring. When cut, their downward-facing flowers can be awkward to display inside, so I like to float them in a bowl of water sitting in the middle of the dining table. *Helleborus* x *hybridus* are often the most decorative.

Red valerian (*Centranthus ruber*)

Red valerian grows everywhere and on everything outside the cottage. It's one of the surest signs that summer is approaching, and I usually cut one or two stems to display with cow parsley.

Wallflowers (*Erysimum cheiri*)

Often overlooked as an understudy for tulips, wallflowers have the most delicious scent, and despite their slightly unkempt appearance, I always think the flowers look charming when displayed inside. One or two cut stems usually find themselves in larger groups of spring flowers. I adore them.

I also enjoy having branches of many spring-flowering trees and shrubs inside too. Perhaps my favourite is mock orange (*Philadelphus*). Flowering towards the end of the season, the scent of mock orange is pure heaven, and the little white flowers are so charming. (There are also unscented varieties, so avoid those if you're looking for fragrance – *Philadelphus* 'Belle Étoile' is a good choice for perfume.) I like to go big with mock orange inside. I want to feel the scale of the branches in a room. I want the room to feel smaller and more intimate with them in it. I use large, sturdy vessels to display them, and they usually become the centrepiece of a room or dining table.

Opposite: Fading quickly, the last bearded irises of spring on display in the cottage.

SPRING CONTAINERS

Spring containers create little moments of melodrama across the garden, and I look upon them as small vignettes that show off the best of the season. Although these are outdoor displays, lots of the containers I create seem to have a direct relationship with the inside of the cottage too, either because I move them into the cottage once the plants are flowering or because they're positioned outside windows and doors to be viewed from within.

Auriculas

Auriculas (*Primula auricula*) are highly addictive little plants. My favourite type is known as a 'show' auricula (alpine, border and double auricula types exist too). These are the varieties that have traditionally been grown in small terracotta pots, rather than out in the garden, to protect their fragile flowers. Show auriculas are further divided into different categories: edged, fancy, selfs and striped, and I have for several years built up a collection that includes examples from each.

Show auriculas have flowers in all manner of colours, patterns and shapes. Some have frilly edges, some are curved, some are pointed. There are stripes and solid dashes of colour. There are those with a light dusting of pale powder across their flowers (known as farina) and those that have the most brilliantly white centres. The combinations are endless, which I suppose, is what makes them so alluring.

Grow show auriculas in small terracotta pots – a diameter of 9cm (4in) is ideal – and plant them in a compost that is generously mixed with horticultural grit to promote drainage. Auriculas hate being sodden, so watering should be kept to an absolute minimum in their off season (autumn and winter) and increased slightly as new growth appears in early spring. Engaging with a local primula and auricula society or specialist nursery is the best way to get started with these plants. Groups like these are so generous with their advice and guidance, and I've benefitted hugely over the years from the wealth of experience they are always happy to share.

Opposite: *Primula auricula* 'Tiptoe' flowering in a tiny terracotta pot on a plant theatre.

Opposite: A potted display of snake's head fritillary (*Fritillaria meleagris*) and ferns in the garden. Right: A terracotta pot filled with mixed varieties of grape hyacinths (*Muscari armeniacum*).

Bulb displays

There are hundreds of ways to display spring bulbs in containers. Some gardeners like to create 'lasagne' pots of different bulbs that come up and flower at different times throughout the season, while others prefer to mix very precise combinations of bulbs together – like a specific coloured hyacinth with a particular variety of daffodil. Personally, I like to display spring bulbs very simply in containers – especially when it comes to daffodils and tulips. I keep each variety of bulb separate and plant them in individual containers to create many pots of single types. I always think this exalts the plant, giving it a certain status and respect – displayed in the same way that a museum might exhibit a precious artefact.

When these containers are in flower and grouped together, they create a wonderful orchestra of spring colour and texture, and they provide a real moment of drama in the garden.

There are some spring bulbs that I do tend to treat differently. I think grape hyacinths (*Muscari armeniacum*), for instance, look charming mixed through something else in a container – particularly violas. I love mixing elegant and statuesque snake's head fritillaries with small, dense evergreen ferns in a pot too – it creates an interesting play between two contrasting textures. *Fritillaria meleagris* planted through one or two young specimens of *Dryopteris affinis* 'Cristata' is a good place to start.

AN UNSTOPPABLE FORCE

As spring turns to summer, the garden's energy is unstoppable; everything is poised to explode into tapestries of colour and texture. This is a busy time in the garden; the jobs seem long and the hours in which to do them short. But while the cusp of summer can seem fraught with work, there's something to be said for taking a few moments in the day to properly enjoy the displays that plants and flowers are providing in that moment. There's so much to see as the garden is thrown into summer, and I've never once regretted putting down a trowel or pair of secateurs to just look and truly take it all in.

Above: *Narcissus* 'Tommy's White' – a very late-flowering variety.
Opposite: A single *Fritillaria acmopetala* in a wall recess.

DISPLAYING SUMMER

*'And now, in the morning, how good it is to
see the brilliant light of the blessed summer
day, always brightest just after rain, and to
see how every tree and plant is full of new life
and abounding gladness; and to feel one's own
thankfulness of heart, and that it is good to live,
and all the more good to live in a garden.'*

Gertrude Jekyll, *Home and Garden*, 1900

Opposite: Nasturtiums (*Tropaeolum majus*), bright and sun-kissed, decorate a summer rhubarb pavlova.

ABUNDANCE!

First comes a soft, blousy kind of summer that's filled with roses, foxgloves and lupins. It's a time when everything appears to be a shade of pink or crimson. A time of gardens at peak flamboyance, birds in peak song and hedgerows at peak fullness. A time when the landscape is flush with fresh growth and the evenings never seem to end. It's an Arcadia. A kind of heaven. This is, I suppose, the summer I dream of at all other times of the year, but it's only fleeting. It gives way quickly to a different kind of summer: a fiery, ferocious crescendo of salvias, heleniums, dahlias and crocosmia. Pinks and purples are now reds and oranges. Flowers appear in vast numbers all at once. Deadheading never ends. The light is harsher.

I suppose, in this respect, summer can really be seen as two mini-seasons rolled into one. And, for me, it's important to view it this way, as I tend to become disheartened later in the season when the garden starts to lose some of its shine. By late summer, parts of the garden have exhausted themselves. Areas can begin to look weary and depleted; perennials that have been growing since spring are suddenly fatigued, looking rough round the edges and dying back. This happens every year and I have to remind myself that it's part of summer's natural ebb and flow, and it should be embraced.

As someone who loves colour, summer is my playground. For me, there's a lot of romantic nostalgia wrapped up in the colours that summer brings; colours that are familiar and make me think of ancient jam-packed cottage gardens tucked away quietly somewhere in the countryside. The lilacs and purples of sweet peas (*Lathyrus odoratus*), the intense pinks of roses, the Delft blues of delphiniums, the acidic greens of lady's mantle (*Alchemilla mollis*): they all transport me from the everyday to another world where gardens are not tightly manicured and vastly paved but are instead jungles of plants jostling for space and flowering profusely.

Vegetable growing is in full swing over summer too: beans, cucumbers, courgettes (zucchini) and salad crops are ready to pick every day. As the kitchen garden becomes more and more productive, I'm always fascinated by how decorative rows of edible crops are. I love to see a kind of chaos: runner beans completely cloaking hazel wigwams, swollen tomatoes suspended from their vines, leeks shooting skyward above understories of salad leaves. Crop upon crop. The mix of function and ornament in a kitchen garden is what I find so appealing; how what we grow to consume can also work for us in an aesthetic sense. Just because these plants provide a service and aren't destined for long lives in the garden, doesn't mean they cannot bring us high summer joy when displayed with thought. I like to mix annuals – like nasturtiums and sweet peas –

Opposite: *Pelargonium* 'Royal Night' dazzling in its terracotta pot in the library.

Left: Nasturtiums (*Tropaeolum majus*) growing up a wigwam in the garden. Opposite: On summer evenings there's no mistaking the fragrance of the regal lily (*Lilium regale*) as it hangs in the air. Every year, I bring a handful inside to enjoy that wonderful scent of summer inside the cottage.

through a kitchen garden, as this helps to connect the productive space with the wider planting scheme. Similarly, it can be fun to mix vegetable crops (like fennel, kale, chives, leeks and cabbages) here and there into a herbaceous border too.

Summer is a time of abundance. Garden borders grow full, plants in containers spill over edges, and flowers arrive by the bucket-load inside. There's never a shortage of material to display around the cottage at this time of year – in fact, high summer can often be an exercise in restraint (something I'm working on). But, despite the bounty, I always try to remind myself not to take it all for granted or somehow become complacent. This is what we wait for in the darkest days of winter; the moments we plan for when the ground is frozen and bare outside. In the grip of summer, it's easy to believe that this time of plenty will never end; that somehow the colder days and longer nights will never arrive. But, of course, they always do – and quicker than you want them to. Surely, therefore, the lesson for us all is to truly live every moment of summer. To be present in all the season brings, and to soak in the displays of colour it has to offer.

NOTES ON
FOXGLOVES
Digitalis purpurea

At midsummer there's a certain kind of light that washes over the garden very early in the morning: it's bright but also somehow opaque, as though it's being filtered through a sheet of golden paper. At this time of year, I sit outside at dawn and watch the soft illumination of the garden; the stillness accompanied by an orchestra of happy birdsong. When I think of these summer mornings, the first image to appear is that of foxgloves (*Digitalis purpurea*). They catch the hazy light in a way that makes them appear almost translucent – as though they were towering glass skyscrapers in some herbaceous cityscape. In those quiet moments, I'm completely under their spell.

Opposite: *Digitalis purpurea* 'Dalmation White'.
To me, nothing says summer has arrived better
than a jug full of foxgloves.

Opposite: Foxglove scrapbook in my studio. Right: *Digitalis purpurea* 'Dalmation White'.

Sowing foxgloves

I grow a great number of foxgloves from seed every year. They're biennial, so the time to sow them is during the summer. In their first season they develop a low, bushy crown of leaves and ready themselves to send up tall rods of flowers the following year. I always sow several favourite varieties of *Digitalis purpurea*:

'Dalmatian Cream'
An off-white flower speckled with delicate purple splashes. Height: to approx. 1.2m (4ft).

Excelsior Group
The classic stately foxglove, which flowers in deep pinks, purples and white. Height: to approx. 1.2m (4ft).

'Pam's Choice'
My all-time favourite. A stunning white foxglove with deep purple mottling inside its trumpet flowers. It can grow particularly tall if happy in its position. Height: over 1.5m (5ft).

Since foxglove seed is very fine, I like to broadly scatter it across a tray of seed compost mixed with some horticultural grit or sharp sand for drainage. I then cover the seeds with a thin layer of compost or vermiculite and water well. As foxglove seed is sown in the peak warmth and light levels of summer, germination is rapid and seed trays can be kept outside from the moment they are sown. Once the seedlings have appeared, I thin them out by removing any that are growing too close together and then leave the young plants to grow for a week or two before pricking them out and potting them on, individually, into 9cm (3½in) pots. By autumn, the plants have usually grown to fill these pots and are ready to transplant into the garden in the positions I want them to flower in the following summer. Over winter, foxgloves largely remain dormant and don't need protecting from frost. However, once light levels start to increase in early spring, they'll rapidly put on new growth.

Foxgloves in the garden

Foxgloves provide me with three things: height, drama and colour. I use them in large drifts through perennial planting where they rise above everything else and create perhaps the ultimate cottage-garden look of all. But while their performance is impactful, it's also brief. They die back early in the season, so you shouldn't rely on them to provide continual interest in the way that many perennials do. Instead, regard them as a momentary flourish in the scheme.

If foxgloves are allowed to go to seed, then you're pretty much guaranteed a never-ending supply year after year, as they are prolific at dispersal. I let one or two do this to create a small, random spread of self-seeded plants the following year, but never more than that, as otherwise my garden would quickly become overrun. Instead, I create my main foxglove displays with the plants that I have raised from seed because this gives me more control over their placement and their quantity.

In terms of maintenance, foxgloves are very unfussy and will cope well with some neglect, as long as they receive enough water in very dry weather.

A cottage full of foxgloves

The colour of the common foxglove, sort of halfway between pink and purple, is one of my favourites produced by the garden all year. It's so deliciously pure and undiluted. So honest and unpretentious.

Foxgloves are scraggly things. They don't quite manage to stay perfectly upright like a delphinium or an iris; instead, they bend and flop more like a giant tulip. But their informality is precisely what makes them feel so at home inside the cottage. They mirror the ways in which everything around them is leaning slightly or bolted together at a curiously disorientating angle.

An interesting dynamic is created with the tallest examples. I enjoy displaying them on tables and shelves, allowing them to touch the ceiling as though they're trying to break through into the room above – you need vessels of substantial size and weight to support them.

Summer is finally here, and the rooms in the cottage can once again enjoy long days of bright sunshine. The towering foxgloves catch this light as it filters through the small windows, and their little pendulous flowers appear to be illuminated, as if there's a tiny flickering candle inside each one. Outside you hear the wild screeching of swifts and the occasional chirping from a grasshopper. Everything, somehow, feels just as it should be.

Left and opposite: The bigger, the better. A jug of foxgloves on an outside table and also within the cottage.

NOTES ON
NASTURTIUMS
Tropaeolum majus

Nasturtiums are not often regarded as the most glamorous or sophisticated of plants; indeed, they're largely overlooked by lots of gardeners, while others simply see them as annual 'filler' material, or bedding, that's easily replaceable. But for me, they have a charm and charisma that's quite unlike anything else I grow in the garden. I adore them.

I suppose a large part of my fondness for nasturtiums comes from what they represent to me. When I see them scrambling up a wigwam or cascading out of a pot, I see a cottage garden world that has largely been lost. Perhaps, in reality, it's a world that never quite existed as I imagine it, but in my mind nasturtiums belong to a time of greater sensitivity to the land and of gardens that were cultivated to be both productive and ornamental by enthusiasts of colour, texture and form.

The shape of a nasturtium is somehow totally unique and yet comfortingly familiar. A flower that manages to be striking in its individualism while remaining cohesive and complementary to everything else in the summer garden; they just look so at home at the cottage. Their scent is another attribute that keeps me addicted: a savoury smell that's similar, I always think, to a jar of mixed spices. It makes a welcome change from the sweetness of everything else in summer, but it's only appreciated when you plunge your nose directly into the flower – something I find myself doing an awful lot over summer.

There is, of course, the colour of nasturtiums too – another attribute for which they are much reviled, but that I can never get enough of – that idiosyncratic orange, which is so full of life and summer promise. But their colours don't begin and end with orange. Nasturtiums have been bred to produce other colours, ranging from butter-yellows ('Milkmaid'), the deepest maroons ('Black Velvet') and even a kind of pink ('Cherry Rose Jewel'). My favourite nasturtiums are those that climb and quickly cover the hazel supports I build for them – I return to 'Jewel of Africa' (which grows to over 2m/6½ft) the most as it also has highly decorative mottled foliage.

Opposite: I'm generally not keen on variegated foliage, but I adore the mottled leaves of *Tropaeolum majus* 'Jewel of Africa'.

Left: The simple beauty of the nasturtium. Five unassuming petals with three petals forming a funnel-shaped spur. There's often a misconception that nasturtiums only flower in orange, but there are many other varieties available in yellows, reds and even a kind of pink. Opposite: Nasturtium scrapbook.

Sowing nasturtiums

Nasturtiums have large, bulbous seeds that are straightforward to sow individually in the cells of a seed tray. There's an argument for pre-soaking the seeds in water overnight, but, in my experience, this only speeds up germination by a day or two and, on balance, it's a step I'm happy to miss out – I'm just mindful that when sown the seeds are well watered and the compost is kept moist.

To get nasturtiums flowering as early in the season as possible, I sow them indoors in late winter when temperatures outside are too low for germination. This means that they stay inside on a warm windowsill for the first few weeks of their life until they've developed their first sets of leaves. (The alternative, for later flowering, is to wait until temperatures have warmed up in spring and sow them outside, directly into the ground, where you intend them to grow – but I'm impatient.) When temperatures have risen in early spring, it's

important that the seedlings are hardened off before they're fully transplanted into the garden. So, for a week or so, I place them, still in their trays, in the garden during the day and bring them back in at night to gradually acclimatize the young plants to conditions outside. This is necessary because the shock of the transition from the stable setting indoors to the changeable environment outside can otherwise severely curtail their onward growth.

Nasturtiums thrive in poor, free-draining soils. If you are planting in a container, a rich growing medium will only encourage lots of leafy growth to the detriment of flower production. Therefore, in pots, I use a 60:40 mix of horticultural grit to multipurpose potting compost. The grit helps to dilute the amount of nutrients the plants receive while, crucially, improving drainage. When planted directly into the ground, I'm careful to avoid feeding that area at any point during the season.

Opposite: Both the flower and the leaf of nasturtiums are edible; they have a slightly peppery flavour like a radish. In summer, the flowers and leaves often end up on the salads that accompany supper in the garden. Here, they are added to a big bowl of quinoa. Right: Nasturtiums growing up a wigwam.

Nasturtiums in the garden

Displays of nasturtiums appear all over my garden, but I like them best grown in containers. I usually use a substantial terracotta pot with hazel rods sunk into the potting compost to form a wigwam. Nasturtiums spread rapidly, so I plant them generously but leave around 10–15cm (4–6in) gaps between each plant. As the young plants grow, they usually find their own way up the wigwam framework, but I check them regularly and tie in any vines that need support. The containers are placed in sunny spots where their show-stopping display can be admired for months over summer. In my experience, nasturtium flowering tends to die down towards the end of summer ahead of a second flush in autumn which then continues until the frosts arrive.

A cottage full of nasturtiums

I never need a reason to cut nasturtiums for the cottage and, in fact, at the height of summer it becomes a kind of daily ritual. For me, they're synonymous with those summer mornings when at dawn you can already sense the coming heat that midday will bring.

The smallest cups are found to house them. Tiny vessels that once perhaps belonged to a child. I like to display nasturtiums informally – their waxy leaves colliding with the flowers as they tumble from the vessel. A little flower frog or some scraps of chicken wire help to keep everything in place.

Nasturtium flowers need little conditioning after cutting, but I find that the foliage requires an overnight drink in lukewarm water before it's ready for display. Sometimes, however, the leaves merely come inside to pepper a salad, or the flowers don't make it to a cup and instead find themselves decorating a cake. Everything, I'm convinced, looks better with a nasturtium on it.

NOTES ON
ROSES

Rosa

Everyone loves roses. They are, undoubtedly, some of the most blousy and whimsical of all garden flowers, and they appear across my garden at a time when lupins, clematis, alliums and thalictrums are all jostling for that title too. Roses speak to the romantic in all of us. They conjure images of times more innocent and impish – sun-soaked and care-free summer afternoons spent in the company of those we love. Despite the complexity and variability of a rose's perfume, we all hold in our mind's eye the memory of how roses smell: an intoxicating musk that can be recalled even in the depths of winter.

I grow two types of rose in my garden: English shrub roses and climbers.

Opposite: A display of large, blousy roses from the garden.

Right: Roses end up everywhere in the cottage – usually displayed simply in glass jars. Opposite: Roses in a Gavin Houghton pot head.

English shrub roses

In the early 1960s, legendary rosarian David Austin made commercially available the first rose that would go on to become part of a huge collection now informally known as 'English roses'. They were bred to reflect the charm, character and incredible perfume of 'old' roses (such as gallicas, damasks and albas), while retaining the prolific flowering potential of newer hybrids.

I grow several shrub varieties from Austin's vast collection. These shrubs produce a classic dome shape of flowers in summer that, to me, is so evocative of well-loved and time-worn cottage gardens. In lieu of space for a dedicated rose garden (something I mourn often), I mix these shrubs through herbaceous planting. Here they bring a softness and sense of romance that I adore through summer. My favourites include:

Emily Brontë ('Ausearnshaw')
David Austin English shrub rose, repeat-flowering, introduced in 2018.
This is a beautiful rose that forms a neat and upright, medium-sized shrub. Flowers appear like little pom-poms in a soft pink-apricot, and they release the most intense fruity perfume. Emily Brontë was named after the famous English novelist to celebrate the bicentenary of her birth. Height: up to 1.2m (4ft).

Gertrude Jekyll ('Ausbord')
David Austin English shrub rose, repeat-flowering, introduced 1986.
The first David Austin rose I ever planted many years ago, and it continues to produce the most spectacular display year after year. It's a medium to large shrub with brilliantly pink, ruffled flowers. Its scent is deep and heady, and often described as quintessentially 'old rose'. It flowers prolifically in my garden for months on end. Height: up to 1.1m (3½ft).

Scepter'd Isle ('Ausland')
David Austin English shrub rose, repeat-flowering, introduced 1996.
A classic. This is a medium-sized shrub with beautiful, cup-shaped, light pink flowers and a powerful woody, myrrh perfume. The name of the rose was taken from a speech given by John of Gaunt in Shakespeare's *Richard III* in which he professes his love of England. Height: up to 1.2m (4ft).

The Mayflower ('Austilly')
David Austin English shrub rose, repeat-flowering, introduced 2001.
A more recent introduction into my garden, this is an upright, medium-sized shrub with light pink, soufflé-like flowers. Its scent is fruity and warm, but slightly more subtle than that of others. Height: up to 1.1m (3½ft).

Opposite: Floating roses from the garden.
From left to right along each row: Jude
the Obscure ('Ausjo'), Constance Spry
('Ausfirst'), Roald Dahl ('Ausowlish'),
Emily Brontë ('Ausearnshaw'), Wollerton
Old Hall ('Ausblanket'), Boscobel
('Auscousin'), 'Albertine' and, finally,
a pleasant but unidentified pale yellow
rose that I inherited with the garden.

Climbing and rambling roses

I grow a handful of climbing and rambling roses in my garden that are once-flowering only. This means that their displays come in one massive hit in early summer. David Austin's Constance Spry ('Ausfirst') was the first climber that I planted up a wall of the cottage and it remains one of my all-time favourites. The flowers are just perfect in every way: elegantly cup-shaped, a kind of mid-pink, and doused in an exhilaratingly warm and earthy perfume that I dream of in midwinter. There's something quite magical about this rose that comes in part, I think, from the fact that it only puts on the briefest of displays once a year. It's aloof and secretive, and there's an anticipation of its arrival followed by an urgency to enjoy it while it lasts.

I like to grow the rambling rose 'Albertine' up an archway. Again, it's another once-flowering variety, but it seems to hang around for me slightly longer than Constance Spry. The petals are loose and informal, giving it a wonderfully dishevelled look – as though it's just woken up and been caught on the hop. It's a kind of light pink to apricot with a very strong perfume.

Rose housekeeping

Any new rose I introduce into the garden is bought as a bare-root shrub in winter via mail order. These roses are young plants with vigorous and uninhibited root systems that are dug from the ground in the dormant season. In contrast, container-grown specimens, available year-round at garden centres, have spent their whole lives in a pot, and will have a restricted and far less mature root development.

Roses require some ongoing care in order to thrive. In winter, my English shrub roses are all hard pruned. This pruning is necessary because it stimulates vigorous new growth without the plants becoming too leggy. At the same time, I also prune my climbing roses to remove any stems that are growing away from their supports and to tidy up their overall shape. Ingrained in my mind are the three time-honoured principles of rose pruning:

- Prune in winter before new growth starts in spring.
- Remove anything that looks dead, damaged or weak.
- Remove any foliage.

When pruning shrub roses, the aim is to achieve an attractive dome shape. For young specimens (one to two years old), this means cutting all stems back by about a third and completely removing those that are growing at angles that don't look attractive when the plant is viewed as a whole. More mature plants (three years plus) are pruned much harder to maintain a good size and shape.

For climbers, the aim of pruning is to encourage healthy growth from the base of the plant and to ensure that all stems are supported by the structure holding them in place. For younger plants (one to two years old), I remove any weak growth that's coming away from the supports and ensure longer stems from the previous season are well tied into the structure. For more mature specimens (three years plus), I do the same thing but will be tempted to cut back new growth much harder to ensure an attractive overall shape is maintained.

Pruning always leaves a rose looking very bare and much reduced in size. At first this can seem startling, but I find there is a kind of excitement attached to it: a new growing season is coming.

A cottage full of roses

Roses already. It always takes me by surprise how quickly their time comes around. It feels like only days ago that the first daffodils started marching into the cottage.

There's no point, if you ask me, trying to make garden roses look sophisticated inside. They're far too showy and flamboyant for that. Instead, it's best to fully embrace their glamour.

In a jug, frilly petals in dusty pinks collide with those in butter-yellows like overblown crown jewels. They enchant anyone that passes by. Over the years, I suppose there have been many flowers considered good companions for roses in a vase – like lady's mantle (*Alchemilla mollis*) or baby's breath (*Gypsophila paniculata*) – but, personally, I can see no reason why you'd want to detract from their blousy performance; I display them on their own. For me, roses themselves are quite enough theatre for one vessel.

I position them at strategic points across the cottage where their perfume will be best enjoyed. I like them in the hallways and by the kitchen sink, and I look forward to momentary hits of fragrance as I go about the day. The smell is almost like a caricature of summer; it's too perfect. Too heady and intoxicating to be real. Too full of memories and summer plans yet to be fulfilled.

Opposite: The bounty of early summer. So many roses bloom at once that it becomes difficult finding any more space to display them in the cottage. Here, a group sits on the kitchen table next to a handful of Icelandic poppies (*Papaver nudicaule*).

NOTES ON
SWEET PEAS
Lathyrus odoratus

For many of us, some of our earliest memories involve flowers or moments in the garden. Plants have an uncanny way of imprinting themselves onto the minds of young children, where they tend to remain for a lifetime as images of times more innocent and carefree. Sweet peas are one such memory I have of being a child, and it transports me back to the age of four or five in the company of my grandad. He wasn't particularly interested in growing many flowers, but somehow sweet peas had captured his imagination. It's their fragrance that endures most in my mind. My memory, as is often the way, is of an idealized world: of hazy, impossibly hot summer days where an other-worldly, intensely sweet fragrance swirled through the air and intoxicated every cell of my body.

I always need to find some level of restraint when ordering sweet pea seeds at the start of a new season. I've become better in recent years at editing the selection I grow, but the urge to sow many more varieties than I can realistically manage always fights with my better judgement.

Opposite: A large bucket of sweet peas waiting to come inside.

Sowing sweet peas

Sweet peas are annuals and the first seeds I sow every season. They require a longer period to develop than most annuals, so an earlier sowing is beneficial – in fact, it's become a sort of ritual for me always to sow them on or around Midwinter's Day.

Sweet peas are sown individually in root trainers filled with seed compost and left to germinate on a warm, sunny windowsill. As with nasturtiums, some gardeners swear by pre-soaking the seeds overnight before sowing, but I rarely bother with this step and have never had any major issues with germination. Sweet peas are hardy, so, as soon as they start to sprout, I move them to my unheated greenhouse. Left on the windowsill, the warmth of the house would bring the young plants on too quickly and create leggy seedlings. Once the plants have established a set of around three to four pairs of leaves, I start removing the uppermost pair by pinching them out with my thumb and forefinger. This encourages the young plants to produce sideshoots and results in fuller plants when mature.

I usually plant out sweet peas in early spring when the days are noticeably lighter and the risk of the harshest weather looks to have passed. I dig farmyard manure into their planting holes and support them against wigwams which I make with hazel rods. From this point onwards, ongoing care focuses on continually tying in the plants' vines as they grow up the supports, ensuring they are well watered in dry weather, and protecting them as much as possible from slug attacks.

Right: *Lathyrus odoratus* 'Cupani' and 'Beaujolais' displayed simply in the garden. Opposite: I love sweet peas when they are displayed on the vine. They retain a sense of energy and movement that's lost when the stems are cut. Here, they are scrambling, somewhat chaotically, in all directions out of an urn in the sitting room.

Opposite: A display of sweet peas grouped by variety. If you ask me, nothing smells better than sweet pea flowers, not even the sweetest roses. There's a deep earthiness to their perfume that makes it unique. It's irresistible to me – a scent full of memories and the promise of endless summer days.

Sweet peas in the garden

My sweet pea displays are always a highlight of the summer garden. I like to display them close to other climbing vegetable crops, such as runner beans and cucumbers, to create a circus of soaring vines. I also usually place a hazel wigwam of sweet peas in the middle of the cottage garden beds, where an interesting texture contrast is created between their tangled foliage and the upright herbaceous perennials nearby.

There are different ways to grow sweet peas based largely on how you intend to use them. For some competitive growers, training individual plants up single canes is preferred in a process known as the 'cordon method'. Here, all sideshoots and tendrils are removed from the growing plant to allow only one single vine to mature. This produces the most perfect flowers on exceptionally long stems – attributes required for success at horticultural shows. However, if, like me, you only intend to admire your sweet peas in the garden and aren't too bothered about having the longest stems to cut from, it's better to allow the plant to become full and bushy by encouraging the branching of sideshoots.

Picking and deadheading the flowers is absolutely essential to prolong the display; the aim is to delay the plants developing seed pods for as long as possible. Some gardeners manage to keep their sweet peas going into autumn, but this largely depends on local weather conditions since extended periods that are very hot and dry will force the plants to go over sooner. I rarely succeed at keeping them going beyond late summer.

A cottage full of sweet peas

On the warmest of days at the height of summer there's that moment late into the evening when, still light, the whole world seems to settle into a peaceful stillness. Tomorrow promises to be just as hot, but, for now, the temperature has become slightly more comfortable, and the only sound is that of the robin as it settles down to roost.

For me, those evenings always make me think of heading out into the garden and cutting sweet peas. It becomes a nightly ritual in the summer in an attempt to prolong their display. I cut far too many to carry and lots end up going to neighbours or sit in buckets at the gate for passers-by to help themselves.

For those that come inside with me I like to retain some of the vine. Displayed on the vine, the flowers look slightly more dishevelled than they do when you have only cut the flower stems, but, as I often find, with a certain untidiness comes a certain charm. I want the flowers to look as natural and as unfussy as they can, and I suppose that starts with retaining as much of the plant as possible.

The priority for me is to capture their fragrance at key points that I'll enjoy throughout the day. My bedside table, my desk and by the front door are all areas that benefit from a hit of sweet pea perfume. Nothing smells quite as good as a sweet pea – not even, in my opinion, a rose. It's a sweetness that only nature could have manufactured. Fruity but earthy. Strong and somehow delicate. The balance of everything is complete perfection.

SUMMER
INSIDE THE COTTAGE

Throughout summer a shared energy flows between my house and the garden; an ease with which the outside becomes the inside and the indoors becomes the outdoors. It's a kind of feeling: a sense that now isn't a time for life to be locked up and that anything worth doing is happening outside under bright summer skies. The age and rural situation of the cottage make it feel very rooted to the soil, which adds to this sense of there being an organic and blurred boundary between its walls and the wider landscape. At this time of year, it feels natural that the rooms of the cottage should behave as a sort of exhibition space for flowers and foliage.

Aside from those plants discussed so far in this chapter, it would be remiss of me not to give special mention to several others that perform superbly in the garden and have tremendous potential for displaying indoors across summer:

Allium

A. hollandicum 'Purple Sensation' is the classic, but there are other later flowering varieties like *A. angulosum* 'Summer Beauty' that can prolong the allium display through the season. I mostly like to stage them individually in a vessel all to themselves. The flowers are also worth keeping to use once dried in the autumn and winter.

Baltic parsley (*Cenolophium denudatum*)

An umbellifer, similar in appearance to cow parsley (*Anthriscus sylvsestris*) and *Ammi majus*, Baltic parsley produces a dense cloud of flowers throughout the summer and is completely invaluable for use inside. When cut, its dramatic plumes reach for the ceiling and create a sort of informality in the room that I adore.

Lady's mantle (*Alchemilla mollis*)

An exceptional plant that will freely self-seed in paving gaps and little nooks across the garden. I mostly display its wonderfully fan-shaped foliage inside, but the feathery, lime-green flowers are also charming and look good mixed with other early-summer flowers. The dwarf lady's mantle (*A. erythropoda*) is a slightly smaller form that looks very elegant.

Lupins (*Lupinus*)

Like foxgloves, I think lupins create the biggest impact when planted in large drifts through a mixed border – 'Masterpiece' is a stunning plant with tantalizing, deep-purple spires of flower. When cut, I like to mix lupins with other statuesque summer flowers such as alliums to create dramatically tall displays.

Thalictrum

Floaty and delicate, *Thalictrum* is another of those plants that looks good dotted through borders in groups. *T. delavayi*, with its sprays of lilac flowers, is one of my favourites, and I cut it to use inside when I'm looking for something that has height once the supply of foxgloves is exhausted.

Opposite: *Pelargoniums* – including 'Royal Ascot' (front left) and 'Lemon Fizz' (front right) – in jars. Right: A favourite summer container scheme with two annuals: California bluebell (*Phacelia campanularia*) and *Bidens ferulifolia* 'Golden Eye Improved'.

SUMMER CONTAINERS

I look upon summer containers like little flourishes around the garden – similar, in many respects, to the way that a chef might place a decorative garnish on a plate to finish their dish. They're superfluous – that extra slice of cake that's wanted rather than needed – but in their extravagance they elevate the garden.

Above: *Pelargonium* 'Royal Night', which gloriously flowers for months in summer, on a table in the garden.

Pelargoniums

Pelargoniums suffer from something of an identity crisis. Their common name is, rather unhelpfully, 'geranium' which often causes confusion because pelargoniums don't belong to the *Geranium* genus. The mix up appears to stem from the 17th century when pelargoniums were first introduced to Europe and thought to resemble the geraniums that botanists were already familiar with. While it's true that the two do share similar-looking flowers and foliage, their differences are substantial.

Geraniums are robust perennial plants. Most often, they form spreading clumps across the garden and require little attention to thrive. They're sometimes referred to as 'hardy geraniums' to differentiate them from pelargoniums ('Rozanne' is a classic example). Pelargoniums are tender and, as such, are most often sold (under the name geranium) as summer annuals in garden centres.

Geranium flowers have five identical petals that fan out like little saucers, whereas pelargoniums have two upper petals which are different to the three below – notable for their distinct lack of symmetry.

Broadly, I display three types of pelargoniums in pots: decorative, unique and zonal.

Decorative and unique pelargoniums date back to the 18th century and are a large group that contains a wide range of varieties. Their flowers are often showy and their foliage scented. In pots, I display these pelargoniums as stand-alone specimens. They're evergreen plants that come inside during winter and take centre stage on tables and windowsills. I find the key is not to position them too close to a heat source like a fire or radiator; instead, I ensure they're displayed somewhere with plenty of light at an ambient room temperature. Over winter, they require little maintenance other than the occasional watering when the potting compost feels dry and the removal of any yellowing or dead leaves. When I notice new growth – usually for me in late winter – I give the plants a feed (usually a tomato feed) to encourage flower production. Conventional wisdom suggests that these pelargoniums should be cut back over winter by about a third to keep the plants compact, but I'm very fond of leggy specimens, so I generally leave them to grow on long, winding stems.

Zonal pelargoniums are the type that most gardeners are used to seeing in garden centres and nurseries across spring and summer. They have rounded leaves and produce clusters of flowers on long stems. I display these pelargoniums in groups in large pots. I mostly treat them as annual displays, but will attempt to preserve any containers that look particularly show-stopping over winter by bringing them inside. Pelargoniums aren't inherently thirsty plants and will survive some summer neglect; however, care should be taken to ensure that the containers don't dry out completely.

Pelargoniums have a long history of indoor display; they were the height of good taste for wealthy Victorians who displayed them arranged in groups in conservatories and garden rooms. Although they have dipped in and out of fashion ever since, pelargoniums remain some of the most enigmatic plants to have around the home and, to me, they bring a certain elegance and sophistication to rooms that other plants find difficult to match.

Mixed summer containers

Through spring, most of my container displays focus on exhibiting one type of a plant, but this changes in summer as I look to have more fun with planting combinations. Mixed summer containers become like little garden vignettes filled with bits of everything that I love – a kind of planting short story that creates drama and tension in isolated pockets.

I often plunge large hazel rods into my largest containers in order to grow climbers throughout the summer – perhaps sweet peas (*Lathyrus odoratus*) or runner beans. Underplanting the towering vines there's usually some French marigolds (*Tagetes patula*) or nasturtiums (*Tropaeolum majus*). By late summer I want everything to be a frenzied and blown-out jumble of colour and texture.

SUNSET

Late summer can, in many ways, feel frantic. It's the last opportunity to enjoy comfortably warm days and nights, to swim in the sea and to do all those summer things you thought you would do back in winter and spring. There's a certain sadness as you hear the last screech of a departing swift, and you begin to notice the sun setting earlier each day; a quiet feeling of reproach that you haven't quite made the most of summer now that it's ending. Of course, invariably, you have, but in those moments, as it starts to slip away, you crave the summer more than ever.

Opposite: Nasturtiums in a dish by Colette Woods.
As summer comes to an end, they just carry on and on.

DISPLAYING
AUTUMN

'The fruit hangs in ample clusters from the point of every branch and of every lateral twig, in colour like the brightest of red currants, but with a translucent lustre that gives each separate berry a much brighter look; the whole bush shows fine warm colouring, the leaves having turned to a rich red.'

Gertrude Jekyll, *Wood & Garden*, 1899

Opposite: *Rudbeckia hirta* 'Autumn Colours'.

RUST!

Autumn is probably the season that seems to pass by most quickly in the garden. It's a slide towards the first serious frosts that kill off most of the perennials and certainly all of the annuals. In a good year (depending on how you define 'good'), this can be as late as the start of winter but can equally strike very early in the season – such is the unpredictability of gardening. What *is* certain is that along the way, as the temperature cools and the threat of frost looms closer, the garden undergoes a beautiful paint job: deep reds, silky browns and the richest orange-rust are autumn's gift.

Early autumn light has a purity and a sort of mellowness that's lost at the height of summer. In those first few weeks of the season, planting glows, as though softly illuminated by a flickering bonfire, and clear skies bring a cool clarity to the intense colour happening all over the garden. This is a time when many of the most fiery annuals and perennials are having their moment: heleniums, crocosmias, dahlias and sunflowers (*Helianthus*) create blazing displays as the days slowly start to shorten, and, all across the garden, there's a sense that it's giving one last performance before its annual retreat.

Opposite: Zinnias, rudbeckias and French marigolds (*Tagetes patula*) on the windowsill as summer turns to autumn.

Above: Autumn scrapbook. Below: *Zinnia haageana* 'Jazzy Mixture'. Opposite: The simplest of pleasures – a cup of cosmos on a dark and blustery autumn afternoon. There's nothing overly complicated or fussy about a display like this; the flowers speak for themselves.

Later in the season, we are sometimes tempted to cut back perennials as soon as the temperature starts to drop and plants begin to look a bit subdued, but the colour, texture and structural value of some faded perennials in the autumn and winter garden should not be underestimated. In autumn, if left in the ground, the nutmeg-coloured seedheads of Turkish sage (*Phlomis russeliana*) look extremely decorative and provide welcome interest. Rudbeckias and heleniums have much the same effect, leaving behind cones of beautiful, chocolate-coloured seedheads that look particularly effective rising through ornamental grasses. Inside, these seedheads are an excellent material for autumn display. This is the time of year when we adjust our expectations of what we can display inside. We leave the blousy bounty of spring and summer behind and look towards a more sober, but still very beautiful, palette of cut flowers.

All around me in Somerset, some of my favourite outdoor autumn displays come not from flower-packed gardens, but from fruiting orchards. Like walled gardens, there's something about the feeling of enclosure within an orchard that I find alluring; a comforting sense of being enveloped by nature. Ancient cider apple trees are decorated with endless baubles – apples that range from scarlet red to the crispest green – and, as they fall, a multicoloured carpet is created that glitters in the delicate autumn light. There's also the smell: an intense earthy sweetness that permeates the air as apples both ripen and rot; an aroma that's so evocative to me and so rooted in my mind as specific to the area in which I live. These productive orchards represent the conclusion of another growing year. As the sun grows weaker and the light more scarce, they bring a satisfying sense of closure to months of hard work in the garden.

NOTES ON
AUTUMN ANNUALS

Although most annuals flower long before autumn, many of them really come into their own at this time of year. As the garden slows, they often show an unrelenting stamina that keeps the cottage covered in cut flowers well into the season.

Cosmos bipinnatus

By autumn, if the plants have been regularly deadheaded throughout the summer, there's always an impressive towering display of cosmos in the garden. The saucer-shaped flowers bejewel bushy foliage in vibrant pinks and purples – which become lifelines for bees as the colder weather sets in – and add a soft, blousy touch to the garden as everything else begins to fade.

I sow cosmos in late winter in seed trays filled with seed compost. They're left to germinate on a sunny windowsill and are then moved into an unheated greenhouse to develop until spring. Flower buds are routinely pinched off the growing plants to encourage more vigorous growth until I am ready to plant them outside. There's a very distinctive, not unpleasant, smell left behind on your hands after this that I always find very grounding; it roots you to a specific point in the year.

After hardening off for around a week, I usually plant the young cosmos in containers (I pack them in to create the fullest show possible), and continue to keep on top of deadheading as they begin to flower.

Inside, cut cosmos is always a cheery sight. I cut as much of the stem with the flower as possible to achieve tall displays that flop over and land in informal positions. There are many varieties worth growing, but my favourites include:

'Double Click Cranberries'
Very attractive with deep purple ruffles rather like highly elaborate petticoats. Height: up to 1m (3ft).

Sonata Series
A classic group that produces flowers in pink, magenta and white. Height: up to 1m (3ft).

'Xanthos'
Soft, pale yellow flowers, the colour of which resembles a lemon sorbet. Height: 60cm (24in).

Page 162: *Cosmos bipinnatus* 'Double Click Cranberries'. Page 163: A potted display of cosmos in the garden.

Left: Sunflowers parade in simple glass jars on the windowsill. Opposite: The technicolour world of zinnias. As a cut-and-come-again flower, they're an invaluable annual in my garden; they bring delicious colour to the cottage while continuing to flower long into autumn. They have a wonderful naivety – the sort of flower a child would draw from memory.

Page 166 and 167: Dahlia scrapbook.

Sunflowers (*Helianthus*)

Sunflowers are often at their very best at the start of autumn. I tend to grow them in my kitchen garden where, alongside vegetable crops, they have a certain nostalgic charm that I enjoy. As with cosmos, I start sunflowers off in late winter indoors before moving them to the greenhouse after germination to grow on throughout the spring.

Inside, I like to display sunflowers in groups; when each flower has a vessel to itself, they stand upright and proud, as though part of some ceremonial parade. For me, sunflowers are all about having fun; there's nothing remotely serious or particularly refined about them – they're to be enjoyed for their sheer brashness.

I usually experiment by growing different varieties every year, but some constant favourites include cultivars of *Helianthus annuus* and *H. debilis*:

H. annuus 'Claret'	*H. annuus* 'Magic Roundabout'	*H. debilis* 'Vanilla Ice'
A deliciously deep red-wine flower held on a long stem. Height: 1–1.5m (3–5ft).	Small flowers with concentric rings of burned yellow and maroon. Height: 1.8m (6ft).	A prolific variety with creamy flowers. Height: 1.2m (4ft).

Zinnias

Zinnias are perhaps my favourite annual. They have a certain exotic feel that, as is the case with sunflowers, might never be described as elegant and refined but is nonetheless thrilling to me. I grow them mostly to display indoors, but they also provide an enchanting show outside. Sometimes I'll experiment with mixing zinnias through early autumn perennials like heleniums and echinaceas, but most often I grow them in containers where they can shine in a space all to themselves.

Zinnias are thirsty plants that can easily suffer in the driest weather of early autumn (with the risk enhanced when they are grown in containers), so it's important to keep on top of watering to prolong flowering. Deadheading the spent flowers, or simply cutting them for display indoors, also encourages increased flower production all the way until the first substantial frosts. Like cosmos, it's a good idea to regularly pinch out the growing tips of young plants to encourage bushier growth from the sides of the stems; this gives the plants a fuller, more bountiful appearance and stops them becoming leggy on single stalks, which, when displayed in containers, is not often attractive.

Inside, the arrival of zinnias in the brightest reds, oranges, pinks, yellows and greens brings splashes of joy across the cottage – something that becomes ever more sought after as autumn progresses and colour in both the garden and the surrounding landscape starts to retreat. Multicoloured handfuls informally displayed in a favourite jug are how I like them best – effervescent in their simplicity. There are many wonderful varieties to try, but my favourites include:

Z. haageana 'Aztec Sunset'	*Z. elegans* 'Envy'	*Z.* Oklahoma Mix
Double, tagetes-like flowers in burned oranges and reds. Height: 60cm (24in).	Delicious lime-green flowers in an utterly perfect pom-pom shape. Height: 60cm (24in).	Attractive, cushion-like flowers in a kaleidoscope of colours. Height: 90cm (35in).

NOTES ON
DAHLIAS
Dahlia

Dahlias are the cabaret act in the autumn garden: performers that refuse to be threatened by shortening days and cooling temperatures – they just go on and on. Eventually, of course, the hardest autumn frosts do finally put an end to their display, but before then there are months and months of flowers to be enjoyed.

Opposite: There's nothing subtle about dahlias – their brashness is fully embraced in the cottage with displays that sing with colour.

Growing dahlias

Conventionally, dahlia tubers are lifted from the ground once flowering has finished and stored over winter to protect them from harsh frosts and sustained wet weather. However, depending on where you live, this isn't always strictly necessary. In the south of England, I can often get away with leaving the tubers in the ground throughout winter without any substantial losses the following summer. That said, I'll often lift a fair few tubers simply to rearrange a display in the garden the following year. You are the best judge of whether tubers will survive a winter in the ground in your garden, but if you're in any doubt, the best answer is always to lift.

In winter, lifted tubers should be stored in a cool, dark place and where, crucially, there's good air circulation (I have lost many more tubers to rot due to bad storage than I have to freezing conditions when left in the ground). Excess soil is removed from the tubers ahead of storage, and this season's stems are cut right back. I also like to wrap them loosely in newspaper before placing them in a wooden box.

By spring, my thoughts once again turn to the tubers as I consider potting them up for a head start on the season. At this point, I'll also divide any particularly large tubers by removing sections that have viable 'eyes' and potting them up separately. The tubers are planted in multipurpose potting compost and left somewhere sheltered – away from all risk of frost – until the weather warms up further. By then, the pots are usually showing signs of new growth, and the dahlias are planted in the garden.

Opposite: Dahlias on stage in the studio. If ever there was a flower that looks good exhibited in a vessel all to itself, it's surely the dahlia. Their complex shapes and vivid colours demand personal attention.

Page 172: High autumn in the cottage: dahlias and rudbeckias in a little bowl in the sitting room.

Dahlias in the garden

Dahlias combine well with late-summer and autumn perennials where they inject bursts of late colour and drama through the planting mix. I particularly like dotting smaller varieties – like 'Totally Tangerine' or the Bishop Series – through ornamental grasses; it creates an ethereal display and gives a quite romantic sense of movement to the flowers.

Staking becomes an issue as the plants begin to grow. Into autumn, most dahlias (apart from the smallest varieties) become large, top-heavy plants that need help to stay upright. The best way to deal with this is to install supports before they're needed, as it becomes cumbersome to do so when the plants are tall. I like to create a matrix of canes around the young plants which I tie together with string. This provides a sort of scaffolding for the dahlias to lean against as they grow.

Slugs and snails attack dahlias in my garden with a ferocity that catches me off-guard every year. Over the years, I've tried everything to keep them at bay – from broken eggshells around the plants to sprinkling bran in the hope they'll eat that instead – but nothing, I've found, is more effective than going out after dark with a torch and removing them myself. There's no way of sugar-coating this as anything other than constant hard work, but, in my experience, the payback of uneaten flowers throughout the season is always worth it. Earwigs are the other major irritant, but these are easier to manage as they'll tend to hide inside the flowers during the day.

A cottage full of dahlias

No superlative quite does the showiness of dahlias justice. Not only are they among some of the brashest and most colourful of all garden flowers, but they also appear in such numbers in autumn that their sheer stamina is a quality to be admired. In many ways, they're the perfect flower. Perfect in the symmetry created by their petals and perfect in their ability to withstand cutting and then remain just as glorious for a week or more in water.

The best autumn mornings are fresh and clear. There's perhaps a slight mist hanging across the landscape but, other than that, the day promises to be still and bright. Somehow, dahlias just feel so right; you can't possibly imagine there'd be a better time of year for them to be in full performance.

The sweet and earthy smell of the ripening orchard hangs heavy across my garden in autumn, and it's this smell that I most associate with dahlias. The two collide at a precise moment in time and will now forever be inextricably merged as one in my mind. The smell of the orchard hits you as you enter the garden first thing in the morning. It's there as I cut the fresh dahlias and deadhead the spent ones. It's there as I place the flowers in a jug. It's there as I sit in my studio admiring their multicoloured display.

The vividness of their colours and the complexity of their shapes seem to trigger some sort of lavish hedonism within me. I suddenly want to display as many dahlias as I can in excessive groups all over the cottage. It's their nonchalance that captivates me, I think. The sense of them owning their lavishness and the take-us-or-leave-us arrogance that comes with that.

In autumn, there's a special feeling to be had when you come home to a house filled with dahlias. With summer behind you, there's an impending sense of the garden coming to an end, so displays of dahlias everywhere almost feels as if you're cheating the inevitable. They help me to retain a sort of false summer attitude long after the season has passed; a grip held ever more tenuously to warm days and sultry nights. I usually display lots of different dahlia varieties mixed in old bowls and ceramic pots. I'm not overly concerned about creating the most attractive or interesting shapes; I just want them all together in one joyous jumble. Balls of chicken wire, the same ones I've used for years, help to keep everything in place.

Editing a list of favourite dahlia varieties is almost impossible as I've grown and loved so many, but, nonetheless, ten favourites include:

'Arabian Night'
A Semi-decorative dahlia, with dark, brooding, moody flowers in a velvet red. They open into a beautiful cushion shape that looks attractive planted through salvias and ornamental grasses. Height: 1m (3ft).

'City of Leiden'
A Cactus dahlia, with shocking pink flowers that have spiky petals. Looks fantastic in the house. Height: up to 80cm (35in).

'David Howard'
A classic Decorative dahlia, with neat, orange flowers that contrast with darker chocolate-coloured foliage. Height: up to 90cm (35in).

'Downham Royal'
A Pom-pom dahlia, with deep wine-red flowers in perfectly proportioned balls. Looks charming popping up through mixed planting. Height: up to 90cm (35in).

'Hollyhill Spiderwoman'
A Miscellaneous dahlia that is completely bonkers. Pink, purple and white spikes curl in a way not dissimilar, as the name would suggest, to a spider. A favourite always. Height: up to 90cm (35in).

'Jowey Marilyn'
A Pom-pom dahlia, with masses of small flowers in a sort of red-purple-pink. Height: up to 90cm (35in).

'Liquid Desire'
A Collarette dahlia that's a complete show-off with purple-pink petals that fan around a golden centre. Beautiful. Height: up to 80cm (32in).

'Ludwig Helfert'
A Cactus dahlia, with glorious pure orange spikes. Height: up to 1m (3ft).

'Mary Evelyn'
A Collarette dahlia, with wonderfully neat and tidy wine-red petals that fan around smaller white ones. A dramatic golden centre. Height: up to 90cm (35in).

'Totally Tangerine'
An Anemone dahlia that looks charming and very attractive popping up through ornamental grasses. Has large, pink-orange petals with a ruffled tangerine centre. Height: up to 60cm (24in).

NOTES ON
KALE
Brassica oleracea Acephala Group

In autumn, my attention always turns to the display of ornamental vegetables in the house. Kale is harvested in endless quantities and, before it's used in the kitchen, I always place big bunches in old vases and favourite pots to create little moments of leafy drama across the cottage.

It's, to me, as decorative as any flower in the garden. Kale leaves are long and arching with a sort of leathery quality that makes them robust and sturdy. Along each leaf is an intricately ruffled edge which looks more like deep-sea coral than anything that might grow in the garden.

Opposite: Kale, as decorative to me as any flower, in a Moro Dabron vessel on the kitchen dresser.

Growing kale

I sow kale seeds outside in mid- to late spring in a prepared bed. The bed is weeded thoroughly and raked over to achieve a fine tilth before shallow drills, around 1cm (½in) deep, are drawn out with a trowel. The kale seeds are sown along each drill, leaving around 7–10cm (2¾–4in) between each one, and then watered in. With fair weather, germination is quick at this time of year, and young seedlings should start to appear within a week or so. I let them grow for a few weeks, until each plant has developed a good set of true leaves, at which point I'll start to remove one or two to transplant into my flower beds – between 30–40cm (12–16in) is a good amount of space to leave for the plants to grow into. I love to see kale growing through displays of herbaceous perennials; it makes for a fun and disorientating clash between the decorative and the functional, and the mix of textures it creates is unexpected. I find that wood pigeons are the biggest issue to mitigate against (they have a habit of pecking the leaves of my vegetable plants), so I place a net over crops using supporting canes while the plants are young and becoming established.

A cottage full of kale

Indoor kale displays are, to me, as synonymous with late autumn as daffodil displays are with early spring. I find it grounding to follow these rituals of display throughout the year, and kale inside is a key component of that cycle.

It feels right that the flower year should be slowing down and that, alongside this, there should be a shift in focus from the showy to the distinctly leafy in the cottage. I use balls of chicken wire inside deep bowls and pots to hold kale leaves in place, and arrange them informally in a fan shape so that each has its own space to shine.

I like to display kale leaves in the most unexpected of places. The kitchen is somehow too obvious, so instead I place them in the hallway or sitting room. A small, quiet act of rebellion that makes me smile.

Opposite: To me, kale just seems so appropriate in the cottage as the days begin shortening into autumn. It's somehow refreshing after a summer of flower excess – a leafy reminder of a season coming to an end.
Above: Kale 'Nero di Toscana' sitting on a ledge in the kitchen.

AUTUMN
INSIDE THE COTTAGE

As I retreat indoors after a summer spent outside, I want the plant and flower displays across the cottage to be welcoming and familiar. I want them to gently ease me back into darker nights and slower starts by somehow responding to the changing landscape outdoors. The abundance of summer has faded, and the heady days of rooms filled to the brim with flowers have passed. In their place, a single jug of dahlias or a solitary pot of cosmos is enough to lightly transition to this more sober of periods.

I suppose I start a yearly cycle of fully appreciating the beauty of plants and flowers in the autumn. The disappearance of everything that has sustained me over spring and summer comes with a jolt, but one that always reminds me of why I love the garden and the things I grow in it so much. I begin to once again look carefully at the flowers that are still around and take in their intricacies in a way that feels unnecessary, or somehow less important, during the height of summer. And so, at this time more than any other, I want the plant and flower displays in my cottage to be exhibits that can be closely studied and scrutinized.

Some plants are a constant to me in autumn; those that I always look for and welcome inside to bring a feeling of stability and comfort. I've already mentioned autumn annuals, dahlias and kale, but there are others too:

Coneflowers (*Echinacea*)

There's something so enchanting about echinaceas popping up through a mixed border in late summer and early autumn – it somehow feels incredibly decadent. *E. pallida* is a very attractive option for the garden (especially when grown through ornamental grasses), but for cutting I prefer the classic brightly coloured varieties like *E.* 'Delicious Candy' and 'Golden Skipper'.

Crocosmia

The ultimate early autumn sparkler. I've grown to love crocosmia in a way that I never thought I would when I first started gardening at the cottage. Back then, it had completely taken over large swathes of the garden and was difficult to control. I suppose I felt guilty about removing it completely – given it clearly liked where it was growing – so, instead of eradicating it, I left little pockets that I keep on top of every year. This regular maintenance is important because it can become invasive. *C.* 'Hellfire' is a favourite for its deep red sprays of flower and *C.* × *crocosmiiflora* 'Emily Mckenzie' too, which produces orange and red, star-shaped flowers on dark stems. In the house, I usually like to display crocosmia stems individually; each one secured by a small flower frog.

Nerine bowdenii

The classic autumn bulb, nerines bring a last-minute wash of delicate colour to the fading garden. They have a fragility that's quite sobering after a summer of brash and blousy flowers, and I always cut a few for display in the house. 'Isabel' with dark pink flowers is particularly elegant.

Persicaria

Towering, impactful and unfussy, persicarias are all-round good doers. *P. amplexicaulis* 'J S Caliente' is one of my favourite varieties for its extraordinary crimson spikes of flower. *P. bistorta* 'Superba' is fluffy pink and another favourite.

Opposite: Potted violas are quiet and unassuming, but endlessly joyful.

It's not just flowers that become the subject of autumnal exhibits, as squashes and fruits are harvested at this time which also have the potential to captivate. I like to grow a few pumpkin varieties to display in groups in the cottage before they're eaten, and there are always thousands of apples that look charming piled in buckets as they await pressing for cider. The objective is to surround myself with everything that the season is gifting us – to be as close to the outdoors when indoors as possible.

AUTUMN CONTAINERS

Autumn container displays are important to me because they help to add interest to areas of the garden that are starting to wane. Although less time is being spent in the garden, there are always those occasional autumn days of very fine weather when eating and working outdoors becomes an option again, so it's crucial to me that there's still drama and colour to be found.

Mixed autumn containers

Early in the season, I like to display containers crammed with all the best perennials still in flower. Heleniums, echinaceas, grasses and crocosmias usually find themselves tossed together in a pot – plants that perform for me in that moment, but once finished are then transplanted out into the garden to be enjoyed for many more years. As with mixed summer containers, my aim is to create multilayered tapestries of colour and texture, and this is achieved by not being afraid to pack as many plants into the pot as I think I can get away with.

Violas (*Viola cornuta*)

There's something so reassuringly honest about violas. They have little paper-thin faces that exude a sort of innocent happiness. These plants are never going to be the most glamorous or fashionable of flowers to grow in the garden, but that does nothing to diminish the sheer joy they bring me. I don't use them as bedding, but as the subjects of little container displays that take me from autumn, through winter and into the following spring.

In late spring, I sow seeds of *Viola cornuta* – 'Red Blotch' and 'Arkwright Ruby' are two favourites – in seed trays, and then leave them to germinate in the greenhouse. Once the seedlings appear, I prick them out and allow them to develop in small pots of their own through summer (storing them somewhere cool in the hottest weather). By autumn, I'm ready to plant small containers with several of the plants – I pack them in to create a full and striking display – and sit back as they go on to flower in an impossibly prolific manner for several months thereafter.

Opposite: As autumn turns to winter, terracotta pots of violas are so effortless and self-effacing. Above: Planting daffodil bulbs.

ANTI-HIBERNATION

I enjoy the finality that the end of autumn brings to the garden. It's a satisfied feeling of closure mixed with a proud sense of achievement at everything that was grown and nurtured. But, while there's undoubtedly a short period of rest, in reality, closing the door on the garden outside merely opens another one to a season of gardening inside. A kind of anti-hibernation where, although confined to the house, the endless pursuit of displaying plants and flowers very much continues.

Opposite: Kitchen shelves – home to all sorts of garden ephemera throughout the year. Here, it's the dried flowers of *Hydrangea quercifolia*.

ROYAL
BAKING POWDER

LA MORENA
Chiles Chipotles

MARM

La China

CONVERSION CHART

3ᴰ	4ᴰ	5ᴰ	6ᴰ	7ᴰ	8ᴰ	9ᴰ	10ᴰ	11ᴰ
1	1½	2	2½	3	3½	4	4	4½

DISPLAYING
WINTER

*'Even in the depth of winter, when flowers
are less plentiful, good room decoration
may be done with but very few, or indeed
with foliage only.'*

Gertrude Jekyll, *Flower Decoration in the House*, 1907

Opposite: A carpet of snowdrops (*Galanthus nivalis*) in the orchard.

LOOKING DIFFERENTLY

Winter: frozen mornings; days that end before they've even properly begun; snow; endless freezing rain. An annual endurance for everyone and everything. A challenge, for sure, but a necessary one that makes the prosperity of spring and summer all the sweeter.

Although sanctuary is sought inside, it's unthinkable to me that a season might be spent indoors without any sense of being ensconced with plants and flowers. But this doesn't mean that displays are suddenly created from bouquets of imported supermarket flowers; it simply means that expectations of what can be enjoyed indoors are altered. Instead of mountains of flowers tumbling from jugs and vases, I seek satisfaction in small pots of forced bulbs, dried summer perennials, collections of evergreen pelargoniums and the odd pot of *Cyclamen persicum*. I relearn how to have patience with flowers and adjust to a slower, more moderate approach to displaying plants that is, in many ways, a welcome breath of fresh air.

Opposite: A dish of floating hellebores in late winter.

Opposite: Forced rhubarb displayed in a little alcove. It's so thrilling to me to see fruit and vegetables displayed inside in this way – it elevates them and really blurs the boundary between the garden and the cottage. Below: Winter violas growing in a scalloped terracotta pot.

I busy myself in the winter with gardening jobs that can be brought inside: sowing seeds, drawing up planting plans, ordering spring-planted bulbs. These tasks help me by creating a feeling of continuity; a sense that this time constrained to the house is not only temporary but beneficial too. Of course, in the depths of winter, I'd be lying if I said I didn't occasionally miss a bucketful of tulips or ever yearn for a cup of sweet peas, but I suppose I tell myself that if it's worth having, it's worth waiting for, like anything in life.

Winter fragrances are some of the very best. The cottage becomes something of a perfumery as pots of forced hyacinths and daffodils bloom in succession over several weeks. While snow blankets the outside world, or fierce winds batter the windows, it feels like an immense treat to have these scents hanging heavy inside. The thrill of these perfumes is addictive: every time a bowl of hyacinths flowers in midwinter, I always regret having not planted more of them in autumn. Perhaps I'm greedy, but life is too short to carelessly deprive yourself of flowers.

NOTES ON
CATKINS

A group of catkins cascading from twisting branches in an old pot is such a gloriously effortless sight in the deepest depths of winter. Uncomplicated and honest, these displays represent the brutal simplicity of the winter landscape, and they create an attachment to the outside world at a time when that is increasingly difficult to achieve.

You notice an ever-so-slight change to the hedgerows around midwinter as, very slowly, the swollen buds of hazel (*Corylus avellana*) start to emerge. They're tight, closed and dense at first, but gradually open into slender ribbons of pollen-packed flowers that sway in the wind. Hazel catkins are the most ubiquitous around me, but other trees produce them too – like alder (*Alnus glutinosa*) and silver birch (*Betula pendula*).

The hazel catkin is a curious colour: a kind of mustard-yellow that in some lights also looks lime-green. It's a colour that somehow feels so right for this time of year; a delicate, painterly brushstroke that shines without being too intense against a landscape that has largely become monochrome. They're fragile flowers that release a yellow cloud of pollen with the slightest of movements (this is something to keep in mind when displaying them indoors if you suffer from any pollen-related allergies or have an aversion to occasionally wiping surfaces where it may have fallen), but, for me, their brittleness is all part of their charm. They're survivors after all: little soldiers that brave the most objectionable of conditions.

There are, of course, other winter-flowering shrubs and trees that not only provide interest outside but can also be harvested for indoor display. Witch hazel (*Hamamelis*), with its spider-like flowers and spicy perfume, is a good example (*H.* x *intermedia* 'Aphrodite' is a favourite variety), but there's also wintersweet (*Chimonanthus praecox*), which has tiny, very attractive flowers and the most sensational and memorable scent.

Opposite: Hazel (*Corylus avellana*) catkins in the library, displayed in the same frenzied and informal way in which they grow outside.

A cottage full of catkins

I have several hazel shrubs scattered throughout
my garden which by late winter are teeming with
catkins. I cut a handful of interesting branches and
place them in pots using chicken wire for support.
I look for a mix of branches that have both open and
closed flowers, as I think the combination of the two
looks interesting inside. Most often, I place them on
windowsills where they illuminate and glow on those
rarefied days of low winter sunshine.

The catkins stop me for a moment every time
I catch a glimpse of them throughout the cottage.
Displayed inside, they take on a kind of exotic quality
that somehow elevates them – as though they've
been teleported from some remote rainforest and
landed in Somerset. They're the simplest of simple
pleasures, and I adore them.

Opposite: Catkins have a way of catching what little light is
available throughout the cottage in winter.

NOTES ON
INDOOR FORCED BULBS

Where would I be without indoor forced bulbs in winter? They are so essential that a season without them is completely unthinkable. They are more than just a warm-up act for spring; somehow they embody a whole feeling and way of living that is totally unique to a period of short days and long nights. When they have their moment, they are the most treasured flowers of all.

Forced bulbs are those that would normally flower outside in spring but can be coerced into flowering earlier if grown indoors – without fail, every winter, there's scarcely a table or windowsill in the cottage that doesn't throng with them. My favourite bulbs to grow include the following examples:

Amaryllis (*Hippeastrum*)

I always pot up a few amaryllis in autumn, which I display on sunny windowsills to enjoy over winter. I treat the bulbs as annuals because I've always had a pretty low success rate at storing them to reflower the following year, and I judge my efforts to be better spent elsewhere. This also means I get to experiment with different combinations of cultivars each year, which, if nothing else, keeps things interesting.

Terracotta long toms are my favourite choice of pot for amaryllis; their slightly elongated shape seems to work in harmony with the vertiginous flower stems. The pot is only ever really a sideshow, however, as all the attention is focused on the incredibly showy flowers when they arrive. You'll have a hard time trying to choose an amaryllis that's subtle; they all seem to scream rather than sing, and the sheer size of the overall display makes them anything but inconspicuous.

'Stardust' is a favourite variety for its dramatic, multiheaded, red flowers that fade to white at the edges and sit on top of an impossibly long stem. You may find, as has happened to me a couple of times, that once flowering the plant becomes top-heavy and at risk of toppling over. At this point, I usually cut the stem and display it in water inside a taller vessel. Amaryllis last for a very long time as cut flowers (two to three weeks or more), so don't be afraid to treat them this way.

Opposite: Amaryllis (*Hippeastrum*) 'Stardust' in the studio.

Opposite: Hyacinths pop up
everywhere in the cottage throughout
winter. I like them forced and displayed
with their bulbs in vessels, but I mostly
prefer them cut and placed in water
where they can droop and bend at will,
like this *H. orientalis* 'Pink Pearl'.

Hyacinths (*Hyacinthus orientalis*)

Such was the one-time popularity of hyacinths that in the 18th century there were over 1,500 catalogued varieties. Today, having suffered at the hands of changing tastes, only a handful of those varieties remain in commercial circulation.

To me, hyacinths have a certain timelessness that remains unchallenged by trends; they have a decorative quality that is somehow both elegant and outrageously showy. When I see them flowering throughout the cottage in winter, they feel impossibly perfect. They make the rooms feel glamorous in a way that isn't pretentious but is instead effortless.

For winter flowering indoors, 'prepared' hyacinth bulbs are sourced. These bulbs have already undergone a necessary period of chilling and will therefore be quicker to bring on over winter. In autumn, I usually plant three to five prepared bulbs in an old bowl or soup dish, but since these don't have drainage holes, I use a bulb fibre as the growing medium instead of potting compost. This helps to keep the roots aerated and prevents waterlogging. The bulbs are planted so that the top third is still protruding above the bulb fibre, and then I usually blanket the whole thing with moss. After watering, it's important that the bulbs are left somewhere cold and dark until shoots start to appear – at this stage they can be brought inside to flower.

'Delft Blue' is the classic variety, and one that I always grow, but there are others worth planting such as 'Pink Pearl' and 'Aqua'.

I like hyacinths best towards the end of their flowering when they are blown out and flop around in all manner of directions. At this point, I usually cut the stems to display as a group in water where I can fully appreciate their pendulous display.

Left: *Iris* 'Alida'. Opposite: Pots of *Iris reticulata* flowering in winter. Grouping together pots of bulbs like this always looks attractive to me: a little indoor garden.

Iris reticulata

I think *Iris reticulata* is perhaps the most sophisticated of all the forced bulbs. Slender and delicate, these irises arrive indoors like little ballerinas performing a midwinter recital. They flower in soft blues, whites and purples, with each petal revealing tiny splashes of vivid colour.

I mostly like to display *Iris reticulata* in small terracotta pots, which I group together on a table as the bulbs flower. Like hyacinths, these irises benefit from a period in the cold and dark after planting in autumn, so I usually store them in a small outbuilding. When shoots start to appear in winter, they're rehomed inside where the warmth of the house triggers their show.

I like to grow several varieties, but perhaps my favourite is 'Alida'. This has pale blue, oval-shaped petals and electric yellow centres. 'Clairette' is another good choice and has darker blue tips.

Opposite: Forced daffodils in winter – here it's the Tazetta varieties of *Narcissus* 'Grand Soleil d'Or' and 'Avalanche'. Tazetta daffodils respond particularly well to being forced inside.

Daffodils (*Narcissus*)

The daffodils that I force for the house precede the main spring display by a few weeks and provide a sort of tantalizing taster of what's to come. The paperwhite Tazetta daffodil *N. papyraceus* 'Ziva' is the classic one to force, but its perfume can be divisive, with many people totally averse to the sweet scent. It can certainly be powerful, but I'm a fan, and I always plant up a large container of these bulbs in autumn for a winter display. The key to creating a full and dramatic display of paperwhites is to find the largest container you can and to pack the bulbs in. Like hyacinths, if the container I'm using doesn't have any drainage holes, I use a bulb fibre as the growing medium.

Most Tazetta daffodil varieties (characterized by broad leaves and many flowers clustered onto one stem) perform well when forced – *N.* 'Avalanche' is a particularly attractive example, as is *N.* 'Grand Soleil d'Or'. For me, these flowers look most charming when their long, arching stems begin to droop and bend just before they go over. You can install some sort of support system (small, fallen tree branches sunk into the growing medium looks attractive), but I mostly like to see them sprawled out and finding their own resting positions.

N. 'Bridal Crown', a double-flowered variety, has I think, the best scent for indoor display. It's a sort of rich, silky sweetness that's less aggressive than that of 'Ziva' but deeper and more evocative than other Tazetta varieties. Its flowers are like little fluffy fried eggs resting on relatively short stems, and they're always prized in the cottage when they appear.

NOTES ON
SNOWDROPS
Galanthus

Few other bulbs have the power to cause as much excitement, or command such eye-watering price tags, as the snowdrop. Perhaps it's the time of year they arrive, coming as they do in the depths of winter, that makes them so irresistible, or maybe it has something to do with the fragile sense of innocence and naivety they exude as their delicate white flowers sit nodding on brittle stems. I suspect part of their mystique lies in the relative ease with which snowdrops can be bred – a tantalizing prospect for hobbyists and plantspeople alike. There's a term for those obsessed with collecting snowdrops: galanthophiles. I cannot claim to have ever bred a snowdrop, nor do I have a particularly large collection of varieties in my garden, but I do enjoy them immensely and follow with a keen interest the developments of those who work with them.

Snowdrops are native to Europe and there are around 20 known species, of which *Galanthus nivalis* is the most common. It's the snowdrop most likely to be found growing in woodlands and along hedgerows – around the cottage there are huge drifts of them that travel up and down the small lanes and carpet the orchards. It's hard to imagine a more wonderful sight in the coldest recesses of winter; their pearly displays are completely heart-warming.

Growing snowdrops
Snowdrops thrive in partial shade, and they are best planted 'in-the-green'. This is when clumps are lifted and replanted elsewhere while the plant is in active growth. Many nurseries offer snowdrops for purchase in-the-green throughout winter, and they are always my first port of call for introducing new varieties to the garden. The key is to plant the snowdrop clumps after the flowers have finished but before the foliage turns yellow. An alternative to planting in-the-green is to plant snowdrop bulbs in the ground in autumn, although this can be unpredictable and the bulbs can be slow to establish.

Snowdrops in the garden
I have swathes of snowdrops in various shady spots across my garden that really kick-start the growing year, but I also enjoy small displays in pots sitting on outdoor tables. I'll sometimes divide one or two snowdrop clumps slightly earlier than normal, while the plants are in flower, and place a few individual specimens in containers before eventually planting them in the ground. I group these with other pots containing crocus and *Iris reticulata* to create little moments of late-winter drama that somehow perfectly foreshadow the garden spectacle soon to unfold with the approach of spring.

Opposite: A display of common snowdrops (*Galanthus nivalis*) rising through moss and echoing the way they grow in the hedgerow.

Opposite: Snowdrops rising out of a bowl in the kitchen; they look so architectural displayed in this way. A flower frog keeps everything in place. Left: Hazel catkins added to a snowdrop display.

A cottage full of snowdrops

Snowdrops have the uncanny ability to display both decadence and frailty in equal measure: endlessly elegant, but always on the cusp of being trampled over or battered beyond all recognition in the harshest winter weather. In the cottage, it's almost as if they've found a sanctuary.

Winter days don't come better than those that start clear and, despite the low sunshine, remain bitterly cold. There's a cleansing effect to those sorts of days. It's as though everyone and everything is wiping the slate clean ready for a new year of chaos and unpredictability. If we're lucky, those days coincide with the arrival of snowdrops when the crisp light makes them shine like swathes of pearls across the landscape. There's an excitement that's unmatched throughout the year: the first little flowers.

In the dark gloom of the winter cottage they hang with their heads bobbing; their outer perianths open wider each day to reveal those within, which carry tiny splashes of green paint. So effortless, but so endlessly necessary at this time of year. Just a simple cup of snowdrops in the kitchen is enough to lift the worst winter mood.

I think snowdrops look best displayed inside on their own, so all attention can remain on them. I use flower frogs to display a handful of stems shooting up out of small bowls, or position individual stems inside little glass bottles. I'll invariably have a small pot of them by my side in the studio as I work – something that's both calming and the source of much inspiration.

It's begun. From this point onwards the cottage and the garden become inseparable. Flowers appear inside as quickly as they grow outside. A sense of the indoors really being the outdoors is restored.

There are a great many varieties of snowdrop to choose from – and seemingly no upper limit to the amount you can expect to pay for those that are most sought after. I think *Galanthus nivalis*, the common snowdrop, is almost perfect in every way and can't really be improved upon, but some other interesting and widely available varieties include:

G. elwesii 'Abington Green'
A very attractive snowdrop with broad petals that fan out around the flower's grass-green centre. Height: 20cm (8in).

G. nivalis f. pleniflorus 'Flore Pleno'
A statement, double-flowered snowdrop with a wonderful honey scent. Height: 10cm (4in).

G. 'Primrose Warburg'
Named after the celebrated galanthophile, this variety has highly attractive, mustard-yellow detailing. Height: 15–20cm (6–8in).

G. 'S. Arnott'
A large snowdrop with thick, robust petals and a beautiful fragrance. Height: 25cm (10in).

WINTER
INSIDE THE COTTAGE

With winter must come some sense of flower deprivation. The cottage is never really completely without plants, but compared to other times of the year, this is a period of relative sparsity. And that is how it should be. I'm not interested in buying out-of-season flowers from florists just for the sake of having something in the house; that, to me, seems like a betrayal of the garden I work so hard to cultivate throughout the year. I would sooner display a few twisting bare branches from a local tree than a vase full of roses flown in from somewhere exotic.

I suppose it's about harnessing the natural ebb and flow of the year and allowing the changing landscape to direct the performance within the house: if the outside is giving me very little, I should be content with that, and focus my efforts on those things that will make the garden even more productive in the coming season – research, planning, seed sowing.

Perhaps we've become too spoiled; too expectant of having everything when we want it. I am, of course, as guilty of this as anyone – largely because the convenience of the modern world makes it hard not to be. Yet, nature still works to a more primitive code of conduct: out there, it's all and then nothing, feast and then famine. The older I get and the more years I spend working with the garden, the more I've come to realize that, with flowers at least, there's a quiet sense of satisfaction to be had in not fighting the will of the natural world, but rather surrendering to it.

Above: Snowdrops and fritillaries. Opposite: The season's dried flowers on display in the sitting room.

IT BEGINS...

Someone should invent a word for the feeling you get when you first notice winter turning into spring. That visceral mix of excitement and relief when you spot a first snowdrop or the day you sense that daylight is suddenly hanging around longer than usual. Often, there's an increased hurriedness to birdsong, and all around the garden there are just the slightest of signs that things are stirring. Before you know it, we're headlong into daffodils, and just like that, another winter has been conquered.

Opposite: An explosion of crocuses as winter turns to spring. Above: Pots of snowdrops and snake's head fritillary (*Fritillaria meleagris*). Overleaf: Pelargonium tablescape.

LIVING IN A
FLOWER WORLD

There's always, deep down, a part of me that's looking for an escape. Somewhere else my mind can retreat to when I feel overwhelmed by everyday life. I've created a world in my imagination that serves this purpose, and, if I think about it, I suppose the cottage is a physical manifestation of that. A dreamland full of colour and expression; a kaleidoscopic realm of words, images and flowers. A constant quest to somehow blur the outside with the inside.

There's a reassurance in the regularity with which different plants and flowers come and go at the cottage. A feeling of movement and renewal as seasons ebb and flow through the garden and then through the rooms of the house. A sense that those things that seem important now will soon be the forgotten footnotes of tomorrow. Thanks to their transience, nothing has taught me in quite the same way as plants and flowers how to enjoy the present and fully immerse myself in the here and now.

Everything that I display inside is really a celebration of today. After all, the present is the only thing that's guaranteed, and the flowers and plants the garden gives me right now are all I can be certain of. Some days, there may be too much choice; other days, there may be very little. But really, it doesn't matter what fills the jugs, bowls and vases throughout the cottage. It doesn't matter if it's the most perfect roses or the simplest little primrose; both remind me to exist only in this moment.

Opposite, above left: *Euphorbia characias* subsp. *wulfenii* in early spring. Above right: A selection of viola flowers. Below left: Coneflowers (*Echinacea*) in the cottage garden. Below right: A bowl of nasturtiums (*Tropaeolum majus*).

Displaying plants and flowers in the cottage reminds me to enjoy the house on those occasions when I'm not fully happy with how the garden is performing, or I'm restless to change something inside. I don't think there's ever been a moment when I've sat back and thought that, on balance, I'm more happy than not with how everything is looking. Somehow, the garden and cottage never seem finished to me; there's never a sense in my mind that I've fully captured everything that swirls through my imagination. It's a sort of constant battle I have with myself: planting combinations could be better, or more thoughtful; this wall would look better if it had different art on it, or perhaps if it were a different colour; that potted display would have looked better if only I'd done it differently. I can't ever accept that this is as good as it gets.

But as I get older, I'm learning, slowly, to accept that this is just a part of who I am. I'm too seduced by ideas. My mind runs too quickly. There's never enough time or space to do everything that I want to do. A whole lifetime is probably not enough. And while that thought used to scare me, now it comes with a greater sense of pragmatism.

It's fine never to be totally satisfied. It's okay to be self-critical. But those voices shouldn't detract from the enjoyment of now. Things may evolve in the future – plants may come and go, and the cottage may look different – but right now these flowers, these objects, this cottage and its garden are a result of everything that's made me up until this moment. Somehow, they coalesce in wonderful chaos to create my flower world.

Opposite, above left: Strawflowers (*Xerochrysum bracteatum*) picked in autumn.
Above right: Pelargoniums brought inside ahead of the first frosts.
Below left: Hardy geraniums in the garden in early summer.
Below right: Garden postcard collection.

Overleaf, left: Baltic parsley (*Cenolophium denudatum*) in a bedroom of the cottage. Right: Icelandic poppies (*Papaver nudicaule*) in the sitting room.

INDEX

Page numbers in *italics* indicate illustration captions.

ACKNOWLEDGEMENTS

I owe a great deal to all the friends and family who have supported me during the writing and putting together of this book. Firstly, to my mum, dad and brothers, whose belief in everything I do is the biggest source of encouragement and comfort – thank you. A heartfelt thank you to my inspirational grandparents whose garden is the first I really remember. To Carlos, Michael and Beth, thank you for your help in Norfolk and Cornwall. A huge thank you to Alison – my publisher – who has shown such incredible faith in me and this project, and to Jonathan too – you have really brought everything to life with such a thoughtful design. Sybella and Caroline – thank you for your expert editing! To Colette and George, thank you for making the most beautiful vessels and understanding me so well. Nigel, Barbara, Alex, Kat, Laura and Dave – thank you for all of your support. Vivienne and Sue C – your constant encouragement kept me going. Sue V – thank you for being so generous with your own garden. A massive thank you to everybody's incredibly kind and generous comments and messages on Instagram; I don't ever feel as though I deserve it.

Finally, Dan. No thank you could ever be enough to repay your love and support. For patiently listening to all my ideas, for all the trips back and forth between London and Somerset, for managing a thousand spinning plates, for just making everything work; I am forever grateful.

Page 1: The late-spring garden: alliums, foxgloves and chives planted informally through summer perennials which are just starting to establish. Page 2: Early summer is a time of peak display in the cottage. Here, roses from the garden sit next to leggy pelargoniums on a table in the library. Page 5: Pelargoniums in a little window recess in the hallway.

First published in Great Britain in 2024 by
Mitchell Beazley, an imprint of
Octopus Publishing Group Ltd,
Carmelite House,
50 Victoria Embankment,
London EC4Y 0DZ
www.octopusbooks.co.uk

An Hachette UK Company www.hachette.co.uk

Text and photography copyright © Sean A Pritchard 2024

Distributed in the US by Hachette Book Group,
1290 Avenue of the Americas, 4th and 5th Floors,
New York, NY 10104

Distributed in Canada by Canadian Manda Group,
664 Annette St.,Toronto, Ontario,
Canada, M6S 2C8

ISBN 978 1 78472 885 4

A CIP catalogue record for this book is available from the British Library.

Printed and bound in China
10 9 8 7 6 5 4 3 2 1

Publisher: Alison Starling
Creative Director: Jonathan Christie
Senior Managing Editor: Sybella Stephens
Copy Editor: Caroline West
Senior Production Manager: Katherine Hockley

MIX
Paper | Supporting responsible forestry
FSC® C008047
www.fsc.org